Contents

About the Author   2

  Stuart Haining

Chapter 1

  My Financial Background

Chapter 2

  Introduction to the Pension Pantomime

Chapter 3

  The UK Financial Services Sector

Chapter 4

  UK Pensions vs the World

Chapter 5

  My Pension Experiences

Chapter 6

  How have my various pensions performed?

Chapter 7

  How do other Investments Compare?

Chapter 8

  What can I do with my pension money?

Chapter 9

  Talking of Complications!

Chapter 10

  Advisor Problems

Chapter 11
   What Did I Decide to Do Next?
Chapter 12
   What are Annuities?
Chapter 13
   Enhanced Annuities
Chapter 14
   Possible Annuity Scenarios?
   Self-Investing
   Using a Pension Instead
   Pension + Self-Management
Chapter 15
   Other Lessons Learned
Chapter 16
   The Future
Chapter 17
   Summary

   Footnote

Bite-Sized Public Affairs Books	46
Bite-Sized Books Catalogue	48

A Bite-Sized Business Book

The Great Pension Pantomime

It's All a Scam – Oh Yes it Is – Oh No It Isn't

Stuart Haining ACIB, MCIM

Published by Bite-Sized Books Ltd 2019
©Stuart Haining 2019

The moral right of Stuart Haining to be identified as the author of this work has been asserted by him in accordance with the Copyright, Designs and Patents Act 1988
Cover images: The Wolf of Wall Street; Dallas; Richie Rich; Brewster's Millions – all available online

ISBN: 9781074954819

Bite-Sized Books Ltd Cleeve Road, Goring RG8 9BJ UK
information@bite-sizedbooks.com
Registered in the UK. Company Registration No: 9395379

Although the publisher, editors and authors have used reasonable care in preparing this book, the information it contains is distributed as is and without warranties of any kind. This book is not intended as legal, financial, social or technical advice and not all recommendations may be suitable for your situation. Professional advisors should be consulted as needed. Neither the publisher nor the author shall be liable for any costs, expenses or damages resulting from use of or reliance on the information contained in this book.

Important Note about the Book Cover

The author has chosen a beanstalk and pantomime theme as representative of both the hoped for growth inherent within a pension plan and the fact that the whole process seems something of a pantomime with other people's money. The fictional characters and actors featured on our imaginary pantomime poster (Copyright owners' rights acknowledged) do of course have nothing to do with either pensions provision or the contents and views of our book – they are merely recognisable characters associated with money in its various guises and we commend you to purchase or rent the excellent films and programmes they represent (*Dallas, Richie Rich, Brewster's Millions* and *The Wolf of Wall Street*) as they too can teach valuable lessons about managing money, plus they're a lot of fun.

About the Author

Stuart Haining

Stuart Haining is an part-time Entrepreneur, Investor and Author and a former award winning Marketer/Banker. He lives with his long suffering wife and daughter in Northamptonshire where in his spare time he can be found writing "cheeky little books*" about finance, cars and e-commerce.

Many years ago Stuart set himself the challenge of being financially independent by the age of 50 so he could, literally, quit work on a whim – if his bosses wound him up just a tad too far. He achieved his financial goal at 51, so not far off target, but of course as is often the case, carried on working. Today he is the owner of several innovative businesses, including a carbon-neutral Online Marketing Agency, so he's not retired just yet, even though he could, on a whim – if I upset him!

This book has come about due to the fact that as Stuart prepares to ramp down his business income and consolidate /ramp up his proportion of pension income, he has uncovered all manner of potentially surprising information. He's concluded that elements of the pension landscape are, for the unwary, little more than a dangerous pantomime, but which ones?

Neither this book nor Stuart are qualified to give financial advice (he was in the past) but you may draw useful inspiration from Stuart's own experiences and decide for yourself whether Pensions are the Best Pantomime in Town or a Show Worth Avoiding All Together?

*Quote from a proper author!

Paul Davies

Chapter 1

My Financial Background

From an early age my parents instilled in me the importance of saving and preparing for the uncertain future ahead and it would be fair to say I am generally **cautious** financially. This in turn has led to a lifetime of being careful with money and expenditure, Mrs H would say mean, but then my ancestors are Scottish so we'd probably agree instead on the term Careful!

All this of course probably also helps explain how my first foray into real full time work was as a graduate trainee in a UK Retail Bank which seemed like a safe and cautious move when jobs were scarce in a previous recession.

The Bank discovered I had a **flair for lending and balancing the books**. So armed with success in the mandatory banking exams I was then frontline with customers trying to administer **pragmatic advice** about investing, savings, borrowing and business. In the days before commission payments clouded advice, Bank Managers could be truly 100% honest and supportive of their customers, make suggestions only in the customers' long-term best interest, hence why banking then was almost as **trusted** as being a doctor. Sadly no more. So even though the regulations and qualifications were probably lower then than expected of advisors today, I suspect the advice given was at least as good.

But as has been mentioned in the introduction, my past qualifications do **NOT** permit me to give advice these days – so readers should please just use the lessons learnt (and my suggestions regarding what I would do again if I had this knowledge beforehand) to help **influence** their own further researches before committing their own hard-earned money to any kind of investment, pension or otherwise. Please don't just copy!

On a personal note I have managed the finances for many members of the family for close to **40 years** and have turned **every penny earned into three pence**, which is about as good as the City generally achieves and better than most Stakeholder Pensions so I'd like to think I'm pretty good with money generally – especially as this calculation **excludes** the inevitable impact of cash taken out from earnings simply to pay living costs, so in reality I have probably **turned a ha'penny into a Joey** or threepenny bit if you are old enough to understand such concepts!

With regard to pension investment I have been an active and keen lamb to the slaughter since my early **30s**, volunteering to join pensions plans without being pushed. And for every £2 contribution kindly made by employers I have **voluntarily invested £3** of my own, for almost 30 years, so you'd think that's plenty for a healthy retirement – I certainly did!

I have also invested roughly the same proportion of income **consistently** over this 30 years that is **only now** being suggested as necessary to achieve a satisfactory outcome – so I was ahead of my time.

The reality though is it's barely enough so you could argue that even the current government/IFA advice is sweetening a difficult to swallow pill too much for fear of frightening people. I've consistently invested **15% of my income into pensions**, but if even that isn't enough, how on earth will people manage in future?.....or did I do something badly wrong?

This book then is an opportunity to **unpick my experiences** – I'd never done the maths until now. And if it helps influence just a single Bite-Sized reader towards unearthing a better pension outcome for themselves (with proper qualified advisors' help, not just mine) years down the line, I'll feel it was a job worth doing.

I am currently in the process of consolidating and organising **13 pension pots** (these are the ones I can to a degree manage) ranging from employer contribution Final Salary Schemes, AVCs, Money Purchase, Personal Pensions, Stakeholder, SIPPS through to the very latest Residential REIT scheme and Workplace (enforced) pensions for employees. And in size these vary from a few hundred pounds to over £100,000, so it's a good mix, and ownership periods span 40 years down to just 2 years.

It's the process of gathering all this varied data together, looking in detail at past performance and charges, current advice and of course the options available under current UK pension rules which have informed the book on topics such as Annuities, Flexi Draw-Down and more besides.

But the book isn't intended as the last word in pension advice – it is neither legally allowed advice (as I am no longer qualified) nor fully comprehensive, as I have obviously focused most of my researches on **what seems right for me, not you,** even though these aims may of course be similar. But even with these limiting factors and with prior experience as a Bank Manager it's been a **surprisingly complex** and difficult journey, but nowhere near as complex or complete as all the options available in the full market hence why I ask that readers just use this book as **part** of their own research to **help lead towards**

asking the right questions that get them an eventual solution that's right for them. With so many choices no two people will have exactly the same research path or outcome.

Chapter 2

Introduction to the Pension Pantomime

So why did I think this Bite-Sized Book might be necessary? The answer is relatively simple, despite being a fan of finance generally and an advocate of careful money management I was becoming increasingly concerned that Financial Services was little more than a complex and sophisticated hidden **scam**, and potentially a **far worse** one than the dreaded world of **MLM** Networking – the topic of one of my other Bite Sized Books, *MLM 101*.

But unlike MLM, which in my opinion at worst will lose a participant around a thousand pounds or so (but also has a slim chance of changing their life positively forever, both financially and emotionally), it was looking to me as if Financial Services was robbing most people most of the time so was a lot more crooked than the worst MLM. This is because the amounts of money are a lot bigger (and are people's life savings), and all this without even the same chance of such a big upside.

I say that for several reasons:

- My own financial analysis had revealed that professionally managed investments invariably lost money.
- In the news it's an almost daily occurrence to hear of pensioners losing out at the hands of big corporations and businesses like Philip Green's British Home Stores – and true or not these are worrying scenarios that never seem to be driven by the needs of the many, just the few.

- Relatives' **Bonds and Investments** always seemed to be losing money when cashed in versus the amount they initially invested, even years later.
- Every time I had a statement from a Pension fund in which I was invested the values seemed to be **declining** irrespective of whether the **stock-market was at its highest** ever point or not. And it's not as if I'd opted for high risk options within the plans. I'm cautious so never knowingly picked high risk portfolios. These were pretty standard pensions of the type anyone else might also buy from a reputable advisor, with supposedly good and knowledgeable companies like Banks and leading Insurers.
- Plus of course let's not forget the impact of the financial services **meltdown** on the global economy and wages since 2008 – it's hardly been a great ride for most people.
- But even these sorry tales of woe weren't enough on their own to shake my faith in financial services – after all, I worked for UK banks for over 20 years (nine at HSBC, in lending and similar roles, thirteen at Barclaycard in Marketing, Research and New Product Development) so I am somewhat **biased** positively towards this sector and of course we are told we **lead the world** in many aspects of finance, don't we?

The final straw came when I read that despite the scale of our financial services industry (it is the **largest net earner/exporter in the UK economy**), our pensioners come **close to the bottom of a league table of the world's worst off pensioners**.

I thought surely that's impossible? I need to investigate further.

> **Editor's note_**– It's true, based on salaries as a proportion of final wages (so that sort of levels out differences in living costs around the world) our pensioners don't score well. It was prepared by OECD, a very respected body.

So I decided to investigate further and record what I unearthed.

Going into writing this book it would be fair to conclude my **expectation** was that once the research was complete it would indeed surely be a story of **scams** and **MUST conclude pensions are poor investments** – in short I had already made up my mind that it is better to manage your own money or invest in other things than the Pension Pantomime.

Is that what I found? Read on and see. But before we get into the results lets also have a look at some data about the finance industry generally as that helps set the scene.

Chapter 3

The UK Financial Services Sector

This seemed a good place to start my research by finding out how important money management is generally and then how good is the UK at this niche skill?

- Estimates vary but it appears that the total value of the whole world's economy, taken all together, is currently around $70,000,000,000,000 so that's $70 Trillion.
- The financial services sector accounts for around 20% of this so that's a mere $14,000,000,000,000 or $14 Trillion/$14,000 Billion.
- The UK is indeed one of the top players (and is #1 in some areas such as foreign exchange transactions and currency swaps) and on a global scale we manage almost 1% of the world's money - so that's a UK industry the size of **$120,000,000,000** or 120 billion.
- This means that *per head* we manage ten times more financial services than the average world citizen globally.

> **Editor's note** – Interestingly 50% of all this financial effort is exported, and most of it is a trade surplus – in fact the only large one we have.

So around **7% of UK output is therefore Financial Services. It's BIG.**

> NB. Somewhat worryingly it would also appear that our largest Banks **each** have asset values invested **equivalent to the whole of the UK's total**

annual GDP output, so if they go bust, we really have got a problem!

In short then the only realistic conclusion has to be that we seem to **understand money and are good with it.**

So surely **this must also be amongst the best countries on the planet in which to get good money advice** and therefore build a good future for yourself and your family?

You'd think so.

My thought process was simple – if this conclusion about money management expertise is true then why do many of the asset values I examine, for example for family investments, keep falling? This seems to be happening regularly and almost irrespective of where we invest. In contrast, money I manage myself seems to get good recurring growth and last time I measured my share efforts I earned 5.5% per annum profit on average. It's currently running at almost **17% per annum profit above** what I could earn in even the very best high interest account, so around 21% overall return on capital employed versus stagnant or declining pension and investment values and a FTSE **down 1.8%** in the same period!

So this lead on to part two of the research – let's have a **proper look at pension values, but not just mine**.

Chapter 4

UK Pensions vs the World

The missing part of the jigsaw I alluded to earlier was filled with some timely research, as the Editor said, from the OECD. This is an organisation of almost 40 leading nations (representing 80% of global trade) to help ensure more prosperous lives – its full title being The **Organisation for Economic Co-operation and Development**.

It produced a table of how well country members' **pensions stacked up in comparison with each other** as a proportion of members' final working salaries in each nation – this is important as it enables the resultant figures to at least take **some account of the variation in living costs** between nations.

So before I reveal the pension table, let's look at price parity between nations (below) and if you check out, say, Mexico (near the left) and the United Kingdom (two thirds across) it's perhaps unsurprising that prices in the UK appear to be around 110% (versus the OECD average of 100%) whilst Mexicans enjoy a cost of living that is much lower, so comes in at around half the index @ say 55%.

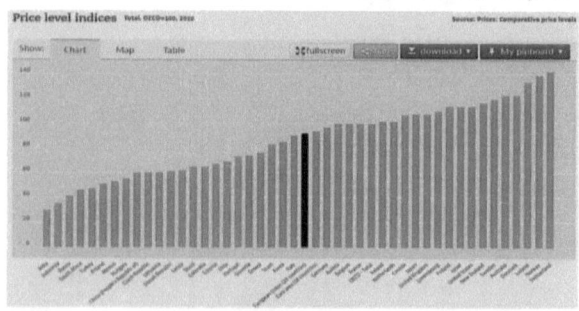

How Prices Vary by Country

From this you'd presume UK workers must be earning roughly double their Mexican counterparts as the cost of living is roughly double here when comparing these two nations.

And because of this I think it's reasonable to assume pensioners would be in a similar boat so due to these same cost of living differences between nations you would hope to receive double the pension in the UK versus pensioners in Mexico.

This is so that after allowing for the higher costs of living the pensions here could indeed pay for roughly the same level of goods and services as you'd buy for less in Mexico.

I presumed this and after checking the **CIA World Factbook**, the salaries do indeed seem to follow this predicted pattern. The UK (at position 39) shows a per capita GDP, which roughly equates to salary, of $44,100 and Mexico (at position 91 near the foot of the table) shows a per capita of just below 50% of that at $19,900. So my theory is OK so far. It's backed up by official data.

So this reinforces the conclusion from the OECD price index data and aside from the thought that we should all migrate to Liechtenstein or Qatar for better jobs (or Mexico as pensioners – which a LOT of Americans are doing) it gave me confidence as to what I was going to see when I looked at the OECD pension table.

I was expecting that this price/value bias was already factored in and that therefore the **UK pensions should be roughly double what our Mexican counterparts are receiving versus final salaries**, or maybe even our pensioners here might do even better to allow for the fact that the UK has so much more financial expertise than an average nation.

But what a shock I got.

> **Editor's note** – Never mind all that, I'm just shocked that the CIA does more than spy on people!

1	LIECHTENSTEIN	$139,100	2009 EST.
2	QATAR	$124,500	2017 EST.
3	MONACO	$115,700	2015 EST.
4	MACAU	$111,600	2017 EST.
5	LUXEMBOURG	$106,300	2017 EST.
6	BERMUDA	$99,400	2016 EST.
7	SINGAPORE	$93,900	2017 EST.
8	ISLE OF MAN	$84,600	2014 EST.
9	BRUNEI	$78,200	2017 EST.
10	IRELAND	$75,500	2017 EST.
11	NORWAY	$71,800	2017 EST.
12	FALKLAND ISLANDS (ISLAS MALVINAS)	$70,800	2015 EST.
13	UNITED ARAB EMIRATES	$67,700	2017 EST.
14	SINT MAARTEN	$66,800	2014 EST.
15	KUWAIT	$66,200	2017 EST.
16	GIBRALTAR	$61,700	2014 EST.
17	HONG KONG	$61,400	2017 EST.
18	SWITZERLAND	$61,400	2017 EST.
19	UNITED STATES	$59,500	2017 EST.
20	SAN MARINO	$58,600	2017 EST.
21	JERSEY	$56,600	2016 EST.
22	SAUDI ARABIA	$54,800	2017 EST.
23	NETHERLANDS	$53,600	2017 EST.
24	GUERNSEY	$52,500	2014 EST.
25	ICELAND	$51,800	2017 EST.
26	SWEDEN	$51,500	2017 EST.
27	GERMANY	$50,400	2017 EST.
28	TAIWAN	$50,300	2017 EST.
29	AUSTRALIA	$50,300	2017 EST.
30	AUSTRIA	$49,900	2017 EST.
31	DENMARK	$49,900	2017 EST.

32	ANDORRA	$49,900	2015 EST.
33	BAHRAIN	$48,500	2017 EST.
34	CANADA	$48,300	2017 EST.
35	BELGIUM	$46,600	2017 EST.
36	SAINT PIERRE AND MIQUELON	$46,200	2006 EST.
37	OMAN	$45,200	2017 EST.
38	FINLAND	$44,300	2017 EST.
39	UNITED KINGDOM	$44,100	2017 EST.
40	CAYMAN ISLANDS	$43,800	2004 EST.
41	FRANCE	$43,800	2017 EST.
42	JAPAN	$42,800	2017 EST.
43	MALTA	$42,000	2017 EST.
44	GREENLAND	$41,800	2015 EST.
45	EUROPEAN UNION	$40,900	2017 EST.
46	FAROE ISLANDS	$40,000	2014 EST.
47	KOREA, SOUTH	$39,400	2017 EST.
48	NEW ZEALAND	$38,900	2017 EST.
49	SPAIN	$38,300	2017 EST.
50	ITALY	$38,100	2017 EST.
51	PUERTO RICO	$37,300	2017 EST.
52	VIRGIN ISLANDS	$37,000	2016 EST.
53	CYPRUS	$37,000	2017 EST.
54	ISRAEL	$36,300	2017 EST.
55	EQUATORIAL GUINEA	$36,000	2017 EST.
56	GUAM	$35,600	2015 EST.
57	CZECHIA	$35,500	2017 EST.
58	SLOVENIA	$34,400	2017 EST.
59	BRITISH VIRGIN ISLANDS	$34,200	2017 EST.
60	MONTSERRAT	$34,000	2011 EST.
61	SLOVAKIA	$33,000	2017 EST.
62	LITHUANIA	$32,300	2017 EST.
63	ESTONIA	$31,800	2017 EST.

64	TRINIDAD AND TOBAGO	$31,400	2017 EST.
65	BAHAMAS, THE	$31,200	2017 EST.
66	NEW CALEDONIA	$31,100	2015 EST.
67	PORTUGAL	$30,400	2017 EST.
68	HUNGARY	$29,500	2017 EST.
69	POLAND	$29,500	2017 EST.
70	TURKS AND CAICOS ISLANDS	$29,100	2007 EST.
71	MALAYSIA	$29,000	2017 EST.
72	SEYCHELLES	$28,900	2017 EST.
73	RUSSIA	$27,800	2017 EST.
74	GREECE	$27,700	2017 EST.
75	LATVIA	$27,600	2017 EST.
76	TURKEY	$26,900	2017 EST.
77	SAINT KITTS AND NEVIS	$26,800	2017 EST.
78	KAZAKHSTAN	$26,300	2017 EST.
79	ANTIGUA AND BARBUDA	$26,300	2017 EST.
80	PANAMA	$25,400	2017 EST.
81	ARUBA	$25,300	2011 EST.
82	NORTHERN MARIANA ISLANDS	$24,500	2016 EST.
83	CHILE	$24,500	2017 EST.
84	ROMANIA	$24,500	2017 EST.
85	CROATIA	$24,400	2017 EST.
86	URUGUAY	$22,400	2017 EST.
87	BULGARIA	$21,700	2017 EST.
88	MAURITIUS	$21,600	2017 EST.
89	ARGENTINA	$20,900	2017 EST.
90	IRAN	$20,200	2017 EST.
91	MEXICO	$19,900	2017 EST.
92	LEBANON	$19,400	2017 EST.
93	SAINT MARTIN	$19,300	2005 EST.
94	GABON	$19,200	2017 EST.
95	MALDIVES	$19,100	2017 EST.
96	BELARUS	$18,900	2017 EST.

How Average Wages vary by Country

So here then is an extract from the OECD league table of **wealthiest pensioners** (allowing for the price differences between nations because we aren't looking at the **amount** of pensions paid in **absolute** terms but the **proportion** of pay-outs versus final salaries when in work).

So guess what?

Despite all that UK expertise and a disparity in GDP of almost 50% versus the example nation of Mexico, pensioners there are in fact getting almost as high a proportion as pensions as people in the UK. We are literally side by side at the bottom of the pension league table, **only beaten to the bottom by South Africa.**

The table below shows that in retirement UK pensioners (and Mexican pensioners) only get around **29% of their final salary** as a pension. We should surely get more as our cost of living is double that of Mexico. Or putting it another way, in Mexico pensioners are twice as well off as UK pensioners.

I was more than a little shocked.

And at the upper end of the spectrum, pensioners lucky enough to be **Croatian** get an enviable 130% of their final salary and in Turkey they get just over 100%. So while UK pensioners receive over **70% less than they were getting previously in work**, in Turkey and Croatia their pay in retirement is **actually higher** than when they were working! I bet they look forward to retirement! And in OECD countries overall pensioners get over 60% of final salary so **twice as much as the UK**.

I was quite simply stunned that despite the apparent strengths of our financial services industry, our pensioners fair **the worst of ANY major industrialised nation, globally.**

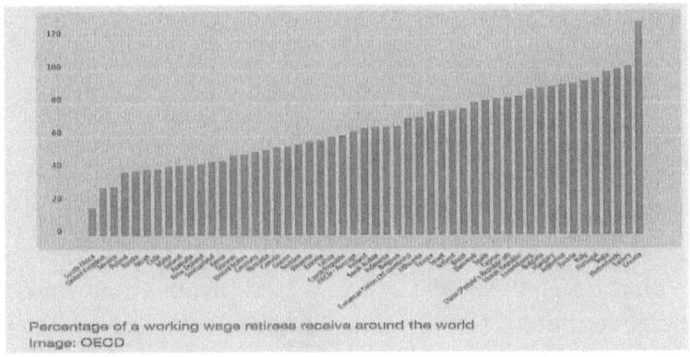

Percentage of a working wage retirees receive around the world
Image: OECD

How Pensions Vary by Country (as a proportion of Final Salary)

> **Editor's note** – surely Private Pensions will level the playing field somewhat?
>
> **Author's note** – whilst that's true to a degree as we have a buoyant private sector, even if we factor in **all** the money UK citizens put into private pensions (which is amongst the highest ratio in the world) our pensioners **STILL don't do better than average, despite all this saving and UK expertise.**

So I decided my original conclusion stands correct – surely there must be something very wrong in the world of financial services, and in particular pensions, in the United Kingdom?

Hence this bite sized book to try and find out some clues as to what's maybe going wrong.

So time to move on I think and have a look at some real life examples.

Chapter 5

My Pension Experiences

I have been paying into pensions directly and indirectly, so by that I mean willingly and enforced (by an employer or the government) for 40 years. Across this timescale I have had the following kinds of pension arrangements, sometimes simultaneously:

- **Final Salary** Scheme - HSBC contributed for nine years, whether I liked it or not.
- **Final Salary/Money Purchase** Scheme - Barclays started paying in on a Final Salary basis for 13 years. I was then wrongly *persuaded* to convert into a Money Purchase scheme for my final year of employment. This is frowned upon these days, thank goodness.
- **Additional Voluntary Contributions (AVC)**- From the age of thirty four I started adding in extra contributions (equivalent to 7% of pay). These were initially arranged via Barclays Life. The company was eventually absorbed into Swiss Re and renamed ReAssure.
- **Personal Pensions** - Arranged voluntarily via brokers for myself via Scottish Life/Renamed Royal London, and my wife at Aviva/Norwich Union. These were paid into for between 1-15 years.
- **Company Pension** Scheme – This was for a company I started and which ended up with 55 employees. The scheme, for all employees, was set up by brokers with Standard Life – this was paid into for 8 years until I was effectively sacked by my own business, but that's another story!

- SIPPS - Various **Self Invested Pension Plans** have been contributed to for 14 years with companies including Barclays, and for the last 5 years, due to lower share dealing charges, JS Bell/Sipp-Deal and more recently Hargreaves Lansdown.
- REIT within a Sipp – This is a **Real Estate Investment Trust** operated within a Tax free SIPP wrapper via Bricklane. I have recently transferred my Money Purchase Barclays Pension into this rather than take an annuity for future income and it gives us the opportunity to remain invested in property rather than shares or bonds and hopefully becomes part of our estate on death rather than lost forever.
- **Workplace Pensions** – We have contributed into these company schemes for four years, ahead of the required compulsory registration timescales, starting with the dreadful Now Pensions, subsequently transferred out to market leader Nest, a public body answerable to the UK Secretary of State for Work and Pensions, so you'd hope they'd be robust and do a good job? Probably not if early performance figures are anything to go by.
- **State Pension, SERPS and S2P**, the Second Pension – I have contracted out of and in to this at various times but TBH haven't a clue what it means so when I come to finally cash in my chips it will be something of a lucky bag finding out what I get from the government after a lifetime of working. I've never had a single week off beyond holidays so have paid my dues since leaving college in the 80's.

Adding all these 13 private and 3 State schemes together it would appear that I have contributed an average **9.1% of salary into pension schemes** of various types (this excludes

Final Salary contributions over which I had zero say) and **5.9% into various SIPP** schemes.

This total **15%** seemed to me to be very high (it certainly wasn't always easily affordable) but recent advice on pensions (now that it's generally realised how screwed everyone is) is that you should contribute **0.5% for every year of your age <u>at the time of starting</u> making regular contributions** to have a hope in hell of accumulating a half decent retirement fund at the normal retirement age. And you keep going at that rate.

So as I started at age 34, I should have been contributing 17% (34/2), if you started (unusually) aged 20, you could get away with paying in just 10% of your salary, but who starts a pension at 20! If you left starting until you were say 50 years old you'd need to start off at 25% of your salary per annum.

Ouch.

My total pension fund is therefore circa £470,000 (so not far off the £0.5m they talk of needing these days) which seemed a lot to me but at today's interest rates (if I could take it all out tax free and invest the cash, which I can't) it would only bring in circa £19,000 per annum, less tax. It's not bad but this is little over half of the current average wage in the UK - so hardly a king's ransom or enough to live anything much beyond a fairly frugal retirement.

So to me it seems the advice that, whilst new savers investing 0.5% per year from the age of starting, seems **broadly correct**, it may in fact be overly optimistic about investment returns. They could need more, much more in future.

> NB. Even if adding on the State Pension (which I can't collect for another **6+** years) it still all adds up

to about 5% less than the UK average wage **now**. So better get a move on and go to Croatia.

Editor's note – I do find it very alarming that even with a rare Final Salary Pension (starting 40 years ago) **and** making voluntary savings of 15% of income for 36 years, it's **still** not enough for an average income in retirement in the UK!

Author's note – Tell me about it, but I'm probably still one of the lucky ones! I'm sure my situation is a mix of factors like the UK cost of living versus my choice of jobs, plus of course how the UK pension industry and government manage money. Luckily I have also got other income streams to call upon, but more about that in a few pages!

Chapter 6

How have my various pensions performed?

In summarising the following data I have grouped a number of products together such as Final Salary Schemes and SIPPs/Workplace Pensions so that we can more easily see the performance of the products that are more similar, such as Personal Pensions in the centre of the chart.

> NB. My REIT is in the process of being established so no performance figures are yet available for that just in case you are wondering and have been paying attention so far!

Values @ March 2019	Transfer Value	Employer Money In	My Money In	Est Tax Relief	Actual Growth	Years (Avg)	Growth PA ex TR	Est Fees	Fees %/T.Value
HSBC - Final Salary	£ 48,968	£ 2,343			£ 46,625	40	49.7%		0%
Barclays - FS/Money Purchase	£ 177,686	£ 26,332	£ 5,637		£ 145,717	31	14.7%	£ 13,771	8%
Reassure -FSAVC	£ 37,892		£ 8,732	£ 2,183	£ 26,977	26	12.8%	£ 4,254	11%
Standard Life -Company Scheme	£ 33,984	£ 7,770		£ 1,943	£ 24,271	17	19.8%	£ 1,856	5%
Royal London -Personal Pension	£ 48,736	£ 33,000	£ 6,500	£ 9,875	-£ 639	8	2.9%	£ 6,505	13%
Aviva-Personal Pension	£ 78,400		£ 46,186	£ 11,547	£ 20,668	14	5.0%	£ 4,881	6%
SIPPs	£ 51,661		£ 35,460	£ 8,865	£ 7,336	14	3.3%	£ 1,447	3%
Workplace Pensions	£ 311	£ 544	-	£ 136	-£ 369	2	-21.4%	£ 120	39%
TOTALS / AVERAGES	£ 477,638	£ 69,989	£ 102,515	£ 34,548	£ 270,586	19	10.1%	£ 4,705	11%

NB. Shaded figures are to highlight losses, Bold points of special note. Averages are of main contributory pensions only.

So what does this table reveal?

Not surprisingly the non-contributory **Final Salary Schemes have performed by far the best** as I was contributing nothing, or in the case of the Barclays pension which I was persuaded to switch across to a money purchase scheme (as these could potentially do better if the stock-market did well!), next to nothing. I just made a few contributions for this in the final years of my employment. These schemes have also done well as they have been in existence for such a long time, it's therefore a great shame that such schemes are pretty much a **thing of the past** and new employees in companies now are always offered **Money Purchase** or Defined Contribution schemes whose eventual pay-outs are uncertain (depending on investment performance) rather than a guaranteed fixed amount based on how many years you worked in a company for.

The difference in performance per annum from almost 50% at HSBC down to 15% at Barclays is I think indicative of the fact that IMHO I was **mis-sold** on the benefits of switching to the tune of around **£100,000 lost** in eventual value in my pension versus if I'd left the money invested in a Final salary scheme. Needless to say I have complained to the Trustees and various Regulators/Ombudsmen (seven of them) many times and have a pile of correspondence about two inches thick. But in the final analysis they all seem to tow the party line and IMHO prove to all be little more than a **waste of space**. But the message is clear, beware the pitfalls of switching anything and don't rely on overpaid quangos!

The **main pensions** in the middle of the table have on average grown at **10.1% per annum** (versus the FTSE over the same average period at 6.1%) so I consider this a **surprisingly credible result which calls into question my whole preconception when I started writing this book!**

Performance between companies has varied significantly from **20% per annum down to 2%** (the latter actually made a loss over 8 years but only just made up for it due to the tax rebates on contributions), which makes me think

picking a supplier is something of a lottery and it probably makes sense **not to have all your eggs in one basket** just in case it turns out to be a bad one – or make sure you **review progress** each year more closely than I perhaps did!

The **SIPP** is probably an unfair comparison as this is made up of long periods of inactivity when I have simply paid in a monthly contribution (which earned little or no interest) and completed no share trades but still paid quarterly account fees. Interestingly my latest SIPPS at Hargreaves Lansdown does pay a **low interest** rate on cash balances (between 0.1%-0.35% pa so circa 10% of the market rate, but it's better than nothing).

Workplace Pensions have performed poorly – and this applies to all staff in my company too (the pensions, not the staff!) but this could be a factor of the fact that these are new schemes and in the early years funds are mostly gobbled up by entry fees. But if it is more indicative of poorly performing funds (as they charge enough but often don't seem to get top notch investment managers on-board) then this is a concern as how can we pin the hopes of future generations on such poorly performing investments as people's core pension?

Stakeholder pensions of years ago suffered from this phenomenon and never lived up to the hype – this isn't such a big deal if people just pay in a few quid each month but with the new Workplace Pensions contributions in the UK now set at a minimum 8% (5% being from the employee's hard earned pay-packet, 3% from the employer) plus tax relief, this is a huge amount of money to be simply handed over to below par investors – it would be better to put your money in an ISA, but it's not allowed!

If we looked at the overall growth rate across all the pensions including the high performing Final Salary and low performing Workplace Pensions the average works out at about **10.9% growth per year**.

The overall fees across the board work out at about **11% of the final values** of the pensions (8.9% if just looking at the main pensions) but what I found most interesting in this latter group is that they have **varied from 5% to 13%** and it is perhaps no surprise that the **worst performing pension was the latter of these two extremes**. The message here is also clear – **check really carefully how much all the pension charges add up to** as even if they sound low, such as 0.5%, there can be a lot of misfortune tied up in the small print with both set up and annual fees, exit fees, transfer fees and fees every time you change investments.

Getting a pension at the lower end of the fee scale (assume it is a successful investment) seems to alter the final outcome, that is the Transfer Value (which is the amount you could transfer out of the pension on maturity into an Annuity or another scheme and you can also normally withdraw 25% tax-free under current legislation) by **about 10%**, which could add up to a lot of money and a **10% better pension in retirement**. In my case, that could be another £35,000 in my pension pot if I'd managed it all perfectly.

> NB. Whilst on the subject of fees I noticed, after the event sadly, that the broker's fee for the non-performing pension was **£5,000 just for doing the set-up** (which took about **1 hour** in a meeting plus whatever time they need for the paperwork back at the office), plus the ongoing commission each year which worked out at a seemingly cheap £20 a month, but remember that is paid forever!

So my **conclusion is surprising.** Far from being a scam, pensions, even the sort you make contributions to yourself, seem to be a good form of investment and in my case beat the stock-market generally by some margin. This does of course not constitute financial advice as A) I'm no longer qualified, and B) who knows whether the pensions I ended up with were biased in some way?, but it is food for thought surely?

So maybe my learning here is that the advisors are right: pensions are a good way of saving for the future. That was a real shocker versus what I was expecting to unearth.

Chapter 7

How do other Investments Compare?

I'm glad the Editor posed this question as luckily I have quite a bit of information about this at my fingertips as I have a number of investment properties, have bought luxury cars, been day-trading in shares for over a decade and of course have run my own businesses, and acquired and sold others. Along the way I have had investment advisors, self-managed my investments, had slightly dodgy *hot-tips* and lots of things in between, the latest being that I'm an early advocate of peer-to-peer investing via the Internet.

So whilst my experiences **aren't a complete list** of the options, **it is a fairly wide list against which to benchmark** the now seemingly good pension performance, plus I have data in some cases going back almost 40 years.

This then is how my own unique list of activities compare in performance terms:

Investment Type (Excluding Tax)	Measurement Period	Net Growth PA after Charges	Charges % of Value
Business Ventures (if continue till succeed)	11 Years	159.2%	0.0%
Non Contributory Pension (Final Salary)	35 Years	36.0%	0.0%
SIPP / Day Trading (Ex Dealing fees)	15 Years	12.3%	1.4%
SAYE shares (if awarded by employer)	15 Years	10.4%	0.0%
Managed Buy to Let (After costs)	7 Years	10.3%	0.0%
Contributory Pension	26 Years	10.1%	8.9%
Bricklane ISA (After 1-2% Entry fee)	2 Years	6.8%	0.9% PA
National Savings (Current Rates 1-1.5%)	10 Years	5.8%	0.0%
Zopa Peer to Peer / ISA (After Bad Debts)	9 Years	5.2%	1.0%
Own Home (After Maintainence)	37 Years	2.3%	0.0%
Company Profit Sharing (if awarded)	25 Years	2.3%	0.0%
MLM / Get Rich Quick Opportunities	10 Years	-2.0%	2.3%
Cars (after running costs)	40 Years	-20.0%	13.8%
Hot Investment Tips	10 Years	-39.2%	0.0%
Average	18 Years	14.30%	2%

The average Base Interest Rate over this period is between 2.3%-6.4% (depending on how it's measured as the measurement periods above are themselves already averages) so the average growth rate across my portfolio of 14.3% looks good overall and has beat inflation by a margin. However not all of these investment options are available to everyone of course, and not everyone wants to run a business or work in a large company that offers share bonuses as a perk.

It's interesting to me that some activities achieved **negative** growth on average per year (foot of table), most notably the arguably legally dodgy tips (from people supposedly in-the-know about what is and isn't a good investment telling you about businesses soon to float), plus cars and Multi-Level Marketing!

Taking a proactive approach also seems to be important or else the average level of fees charged at 2% could easily erode any growth through natural inflation.

Contributory Pensions scored well on this comparison table with a performance (+10.1%) broadly similar to investing in rental properties (10.3%) after allowing for rental income/house price growth minus maintenance and management costs, and service charges, so everything but tax, plus of course it's important to remember that property ownership can be a hassle and huge risk.

I have already mentioned that, sadly, few people these days can benefit from **Final Salary** (Non Contributory) Pensions, plus not all companies give away shares or offer **Save As You Earn** Schemes to staff. Companies quoted on the Stock Market are the most likely source of these kind of benefits although even my own small advertising agency does award shares and dividends to current employees and former staff.

Starting and profiting from **Business** does seem to be a very strong contender as the best way to make money but of course most business ventures fail (**80%** can generally be regarded as failures within **5** years) so it is hugely important to manage your scarce capital and time well. In business it probably is no bad thing to have your finger in more than one pie at a time, that way you can then quickly **shift** your assets behind the obvious **winners** and cut your losses elsewhere.

> NB. In my Bite-Sized book *Profitable Partnerships* I have detailed how over a 50 year period I have been involved in circa 160 *business* type discussions and potential partnerships of which 28 were a success of various degrees making an **average profit of £68,000** each. This probably wouldn't have happened if I hadn't been persistent and had several horses in the race, as I could have backed a loser if I'd only tried business once or twice.

The other investment type, which in my experience has beaten pensions, but again isn't for everyone and it certainly is high risk, is Self-Management of investments via a vehicle such as a **SIPP** or **Stocks and Shares ISA** which has delivered circa **12.3%** overall and is therefore around **20% above my pension returns**. My current performance though (which will probably be skewed by current stock market performance) is doing even better than this at around 21% per annum and **double my average pension return**.

Self-Investment is therefore potentially an investment type that merits a closer look and I will probably write another Bite Sized Book about this called *StayTrading©* – This is my name for **my style of Day Trading**! It has elements of normal Day Trading (a quick in and out buying and selling the asset, hopefully within a single day) but I stay for longer if needs be as I won't crystallise an on-paper losing position into a real-world losing position by automatically being forced into selling and closing a position at the end of the day. In fact the opposite is true – I will hold a share until hell freezes over, or the company has gone bust whilst I wait for my investment to turn even a small token profit.

Dealing in shares is of course **high risk** almost akin to going to a casino (although you don't always need to lose your chips after each bet!) so is probably not for everyone. It's certainly not always suitable as an alternative to sensible pension investment as share values can suddenly fall, companies unexpectedly get taken over/go bankrupt (remember Comet electrical – it sold for just £2) and the whole global economy can suffer from a downturn literally overnight. Brexit is one such example of how even the best laid investment plan can suddenly be derailed by unusual activity at any time. This is less important if you are in it for the long haul but of vital significance if you are cash strapped and need to sell assets to take money out at the very point when the market is down.

For this reason I only Stay Trade with just 45% of our pension assets which **represents less than 10% of our anticipated total income** in retirement, so it's a hopefully manageable risk if it all went horribly wrong.

So the conclusion I think from my experience, and completely contrary to my expectations before I started writing this Bite Sized Book, is that **Pensions are not a scam** and in fact represent a good long term investment, but with some provisos:

- I suspect it's a good idea to hedge your bets with more than one scheme

- It's also vital to regularly and thoroughly check performance
- And it's worth paying attention to the level of charges being made.

So is this the end of the book?

It would be if saving for a pension was the **end of the journey**, but of course it isn't. When you get to your desired pension age and need to start drawing money from your saved pot, you have a whole host of decisions to make about **what to do next** with your money.

Chapter 8

What can I do with my pension money?

Again as I'm no longer qualified to give pension advice I don't feel the need to ensure that this section is a full examination of **all** the possible options available in the UK. Instead I will share what seemed **relevant choices to me** as I am planning in the not too distant future to start leveraging my savings and taking money out to replace a gradual reduction in income.

I have an amount of prior knowledge from my time working as a Bank Manager so whilst I may be a bit more clued up than your average man or women in the street, in actual fact I'm a bit of a dunce about pensions as let's face it, it's the kind of thing we all put off thinking about until it's almost too late!

So maybe my journey is reasonably representative after all of other people too?

The first thing you'll notice as you head into your fifties is all of the sudden attention you get from new friends who **just happen to be financial advisors or IFAs**. These people generally work under the umbrella of a larger financial organisation (which has back-room boffins doing research and analysis) so they can cover themselves legally by being seen to have the best data possible to ensure they give you best advice. This is good in theory but as they **earn commission** when they sell you something (usually either a large initial fee and small lifetime recurring fee, or vice versa) or persuade you to switch, in my experience all that theory is out the window and you generally get sold something that is less than a perfect fit but happens to **reward the seller well**.

If you've ever wondered how most IFAs own nice houses and cars (or their bosses do), now you know – and it could all happen in a few hours' work, hence why they are particularly nice and courteous to you when you have a few hundred thousand pounds sitting in a pension pot just waiting to do something with it. To financial brokers, which is what they really are, it's not so different to going into an **up-market car dealership with enough cash in a briefcase to buy TEN cars outright** on the day – and imagine how pleased they'd be to see you too!.

Pension Wise (a government sponsored organisation to provide Free and independent advice) will also start to contact you along with notices from your pension schemes advising you how much your fund is worth (the Transfer Value or Fund Value – they may differ slightly) and what this might pay you when you hit various retirement dates, including early or late retirement beyond the normal state pension age. It is well worth taking up the option of a Free meeting with Pension Wise, and I think you can even have more than one, usually somewhere like a Citizens Advice Bureau, as they will be paying an advisor with **good knowledge** to talk you through your various options and more. They are also keen to help you rule out falling for some obvious scams and pitfalls. But in my experience they won't make firm decisions for you and will say that's the job for Financial Advisors or regulators, either Free (and reimbursed by commissions) or you can opt to pay them a fee for the advice. This will typically be around £600 and you can usually withdraw this from one of your pension pots. Given the fact I think most advisors are biased, intentionally or otherwise, this seems a **very poor use of £600** to me.

Whilst on the subject of advisors I do think it's still possible to come across some confusing variants – for example people or companies who seem on the face of it to be independent advisors but in fact they are only regulated to **make suggestions from a range of their own companies' portfolio of products**. The rules here are gradually being tightened up as it is confusing but this used to include my advisors at both Barclays Bank and St James Place – and yet in both cases you'd have assumed they had the freedom to pick what was exactly right for me from the whole market. This wasn't the case as they are tied to a restricted range of products, albeit still a big range of course.

Some other firms are also known for issuing excellent **research** papers on specific investments but these are not to be confused with actually giving investment advice – this is the kind of service I enjoy from both JS Bell/Sipp Deal and Hargreaves Lansdown – but again you need to remember that they are not necessarily acting in your specific best interest as they don't know your circumstances and they do earn commission. They are in fact **Execution Only** advisers so they are helping to educate you just enough to favour one of their investment options but ultimately it is your decision, not theirs, so there is no comeback if it doesn't work out (beyond any government safety net of course).

I have also come across people affiliated with various of these organisations who then sell you a advice service for a monthly fee even though that's not a service offered or supported by the company itself – not surprisingly this off-piste kind of activity will rarely go well or be guaranteed to be solely in your own best interest as they are already breaking the rules!

So what are the options?

Recent legislation has opened all kinds of freedoms for pensioners and the soon to be retired. In the past you were I believe **forced to take an annuity** (kind of like a long term insurance policy) with a sub-division of your pension provider, so they kept your money **throughout** from starting saving to death. They paid you a guaranteed pension once you retired, they probably paid a reduced amount to your spouse and a lump sum on your death if it came early, and that was it. No choice, no shopping around and of course no benefits to pass on to your children or grandchildren.

So one of the first changes these days is that you may have freedom of **choice** as to where you move your money and take an annuity, but not always, as I will explain in a moment.

They also opened up the dates – in the past unless your final salary scheme let you chose to retire early, you had to wait until the normal retirement age until you could start collecting your pension, so typically that would be aged 60 for women and 65 for men. These dates are of course being gradually drawn into alignment to avoid claims of sexism and they are being pushed back ever later as the country can't afford pensions, as we saw in the earlier tables. But recent changes enable everyone to **start taking a pension from aged 55**, even if you are still at work. This of course **doesn't mean that at age 55 you will in fact have enough money to afford to be able to take a pension** from that age, but the option is generally available if you want that flexibility.

For some time it has also been possible to take the first part of your pension tax free, which is actually a great concession from the tax-man which may not last forever given they have already given us a tax rebate on the money we paid into our pensions in the first place. The rules about this tax free element seem complicated but as best as I can work out you broadly have a **choice between taking 25% of your transfer value out first, tax free,** and then pay tax on whatever happens with the rest at a later date, **or you take 25% of whatever subsequent monthly or quarterly or annual withdrawals you make** from your pot once you start to draw it down (hence it's called drawdown) and all the rest is taxed.

I think I may decide to take the lump sum on the basis of a bird-in-the-hand and all that.

I don't think you can then shove it all straight back into your pension and get yet more tax relief on your tax free money – well you can a bit but that's even more complicated and I will say more on that a bit further into the book's probable conclusions! This fits into the Annual Allowance rules on Pension Recycling.

Chapter 9

Talking of Complications!

During my own pension research and preparing to write this book I have come across all the following terms, a few I was already aware of but how a typical consumer who hasn't worked in financial services is supposed to cope, heaven knows. It's not an exhaustive list but I will attempt to put next to each what I concluded it means:

Administration Fees – How much to do/keep doing something for you?

Annual Allowance – How much you can add to your pension yearly?

Beneficiary/Nominee Pension – Who gets what when you die?

Benefit Crystallisation Event (BCE) – You've started to take money out.

Benefit Entitlement – Will your pension impact other State Benefits?

Capital Protected Annuity – **VITAL** for your family to get all the money.

Continued Investment – Some of your pension stays invested to earn.

Crystallised Pension – They think you've started retirement.

Defined Contribution – You save a regular amount into the plan.

<u>Defined Benefit</u> – You get known amounts out e.g. Final Salary x50% pa.

<u>Drawdown</u> – You've started taking money from your pension.

<u>Emergency Tax</u> – They tax you this much till they work out a tax code.

<u>Enhanced Annuity Rates</u> – You might get more if you have ill health.

<u>Escalating Annuity</u> – Your drawings out can go up each year.

<u>Escalating Lifetime Annuity</u> – ditto.

<u>Fixed Term Annuity</u> – Your pension only pays out for a specified period.

<u>Flexible Annuity</u> – You can start payments low or high and change later.

<u>Flexible Death Benefits</u> – You get some say re who gets what after death.

<u>Flexible Drawdown</u> – You can alter when and how much you take out.

<u>FLUMP</u> – Same as UFPLS

<u>Funds Transfer</u> – How much your pension will shift to another scheme.

<u>Guarantee Period</u> – Your pension is paid for this long even if you die.

<u>IFA</u> – Independent Financial Advisor – who may be anything but!

<u>Impaired Annuity</u> – Extra money from 1-25% for poor health/lifestyle.

<u>Immediate Life Annuity</u> – Uses your cash instead of pension funds.

Income Drawdown – You have started to take money out.

Income Floors – A minimum liveable threshold to receive each month.

Index Linked – Your pension will increase a bit as prices rise.

Investment Backed Annuities – Pension income varies with the markets.

Level Income – Your pension pay-outs won't increase over time.

Life Cover – If your pension pays out a free lump sum on death.

Lifetime Allowance – The limit you can ever pay into a pension.

Lifetime Annuity – A guaranteed income in retirement for life.

Lump Sum – Usually the tax free amount you can take out – 25%

Marginal Rate – If you take all cash, you'll pay your **highest tax** rate.

Money Purchase Annual Allowance – the amount you can contribute.

Overlap – something to do with when your spouse gets paid if you die.

Pension Drawdown Account – A special account for taking money out.

Pension Recycling – Re-investing Tax Free Cash to get more Tax Free!

Private Pension – Generally something you organise to supplement SP.

REIT/Real Estate Investment Trust – Tax Free Property Investment.

Retail Price Indexation – Your pension increases with inflation, almost.

Selected Retirement Age – When you chose to retire, if not normal age.

SERPS – The State Pension aka State Earnings Related Pension Scheme.

Short Term Annuities – A short term arrangement before a final choice.

Single Life – The pension only pays out for one person, no spouse.

SIPP/Self Invested Personal Pension – A low cost DIY pension.

SP/State Pension – Basic pension for workers without their own pension.

Spouse Pension – After you die your spouse gets an agreed % later.

Standard Annuity Rates – How much your pot can buy in the market.

State Pension 2 – An add on pension to supplement the above, if you pay in for it and don't op out.

Tax Free Lump Sum – How much you get as a lump sum, tax free!

Tied Financial Advisor – They mostly recommend company products.

Uncrystallised – Taking out your 25% tax free and leaving the rest in.

Uncrystallised Funds Pension Lump Sum (UFPLS) – as above.

<u>With/Without Proportion</u> – Money for spouses if die between payments.

I think you will agree with so many elements to consider, the whole pension scene is hugely complex and has perhaps been worsened with the recent freedoms introduced by the government. Particularly important aspects (IMHO) such as **Capital Protected Annuity** and Marginal Rate Tax are **buried** in at least 50 other topics. Is it any wonder bad decisions get made along the way?

On the one hand, yes, these days we have more choice than an annuity (money out) option being only available from the original (money in) pension provider, so these days we can do better for ourselves, but on the other side of the equation it seems to me all this complexity pushes us almost **automatically into the hands of Independent Financial Advisors**, where even the most well intentioned can still end up giving us advice that either unwittingly costs us a great deal in commission or at the very worst can rob us of a half decent pension in retirement as they are not truly unbiased, whatever the law may say or aim for.

As I have already mentioned I was a former Bank Manager and whilst I may not be the sharpest tool in the box, I'm certainly far from the bluntest. I may have failed the easy Bank exams many times but I passed the most complicated ones with flying colours first time and have a decent IQ!

> **Editor's note** – what a surprise….the exam bit I mean!
>
> **Author's note** – I guess I'll have to take that as a compliment!

Anyway, my point is this, if I am reasonably intelligent and **still find all this complicated,** and that's even after working in finance for years AND meeting several advisors AND using the excellent Free PensionWise service, then I can only begin to imagine how complicated and bewildering anyone who hasn't dealt with finance will find all this?

It really IS a Pantomime!

And if my experience is anything to go by, they will be little wiser after meeting IFAs, but they will of course be poorer!

Chapter 10

Advisor Problems

My experiences may not be wholly representative of the market of course but I will list out below just a **few** of the difficulties I have encountered when seeking pension advice:

Irrelevant Advice – Armed with all the support of back-room researchers they often present you with a range of possible suppliers to pick from. We picked the one with the highest estimated return only to be declined subsequently by said provider on the basis of "why would anyone need a return this big?" They concluded "you must be dodgy. Or up-to something". But we were using their own data and an IFA. We didn't make the data dodgy! Go Figure!

Inflexible Fees – Even if you know exactly what product you want don't expect to pay any less for the advice, even if it's a lightning quick meeting it could still cost you **£5,000 for an hour**! But it probably won't be any cheaper even if you try and purchase direct from the supplier. Go Figure strike 2!

Inappropriate Fees – We've been charged a monthly retainer of £50 for over a year by an advisor whose own organisation prohibited such a scenario (obviously we didn't know that until after the event) and we got nothing meaningful extra for such a fee.

Tied Products – As already mentioned even with some of the biggest advisors who appear to be independent it is easy to be misled and discover that they do in fact only recommend the products and services from a **subset** of the whole market – this might be 1% of the market, 10% or 80%, but it's not everything and so you **can't be sure** you are getting the **best advice tailored to your unique needs**. This will of course be explained somewhere in reams of small print that few people read and even if you did it will most likely be obfuscated in legalise so it's hard to work out the meaning, just as I've done here with these words!

<u>Misunderstood Goals</u> – On several occasions I have met with advisors, explained our investment strategy and which assets we have invested in only to receive immediate advice *"it's all **wrong.**"* But when they subsequently take the time to learn more fully about our lifestyle and investment goals they change tack and in a couple of cases have asked to be *"kept informed the next time you are investing so we can **copy the strategy**"* themselves. I don't mind the latter but it says to me many advisors jump into making **snap decisions** about portfolios and types of investment before fully grasping anything meaningful about what the customer wants to achieve in life, so they are probably just regurgitating **standard pitches** used time and time again with many clients. So as an example, IMHO it seems as if two people with an identical portfolio of assets would receive the same initial advice irrespective of whether one had been diagnosed say with cancer and had a year to live, while the other's family has a history of becoming centenarians. This is plainly not good enough.

<u>Legislative Black Hole</u> – I have recently been trying to transfer a reasonably modest Bank Pension of the Final Salary type – so this is one which affords me a small pension based on how many years I worked there (divided by the maximum possible and multiplied by my final salary), so circa 9/60ths x £9,000 = £1,500 pa plus increases for inflation so it's actually worth about £400 a month to

me. Well, because of all the furore about pension mis-selling and because such pensions often have extra benefits like Life Cover and a Spouse/Beneficiary/Nominee Pension (which are expensive add-ons to a normal Pension), the government, rightly, don't want people to give up these schemes lightly and get hoodwinked into a Money Purchase plan or similar. So UK law says you MUST get professional advice at a cost of around **£600 a time**, and said advice **must support** a switch. The same rules apply to some government pensions.

But advisors are now **so worried about being sued** over advice for Final Salary and similar pensions that they simply **won't ever give advice** to switch, even if the reason is a good one, such as wanting a Capital Protected Annuity (to benefit your next of kin) or Flexi Drawdown, which I do.

I tried complaining to the Pensions Ombudsman (Ed: *now that's a surprise!*) that this is a catch 22 situation, that is legislation forces me to waste £600 for advice I simply cannot get (even if the advisor agrees with the argument). Not surprisingly I got nowhere with Regulators who are yet again a complete waste of space – in this instance they **can't even give a ruling on a case by case basis** re how they interpret their own rules so an IFA knows he is safe or not!

> **Editor's note** – It really is a case then of "this is OK, oh yes it is, oh no it isn't" just like your book title!

In short they operate in the narrow confines of their own pre-existing legislative framework established by Parliament and can't even suggest ways to improve their own processes even if it's in the public interest as this would require a new Act of Parliament. In my mind this makes the whole thing an expensive circus at tax-payers' expense, as always.

NB. However, you may be interested and surprised to hear that I **have** been offered the necessary letter **supporting** my pension transfer out of Final Salary and agreeing to help implement it, provided I simultaneously agree to **purchase from said advisor** a **new pension myself and arrange a company scheme** for all my employees. In short, **bribery** of a sort which I would imagine is highly **fraudulent**. Does the regulator care? Of course not. I've alerted them to what's happened as surely that's in the public interest and they don't even bat an eye. It does kind of lend credence to the thought that this industry is all one giant cosy club paying all the pantomime actors and regulators huge salaries for not rocking the boat.

Editor's note – That is truly shocking and a disgrace, but do you get boats in Pantomimes?

<u>Don't always trust a Trustee</u> – You would imagine I think that at least the pension trustees themselves must have **only the interests of pensioners** in mind? After all, what else are they in a job for? And I can't imagine they do it for free!

My own experiences suggest even this obvious goal may be far from the reality. In one of my pensions I was persuaded (IMHO by high pressure persuasive marketing and extra financial carrots) to switch from a Final Salary into a Money Purchase Scheme even though the Trustees and Company suspected it had a high chance of leaving pensioners worse off – that's why they were pushing it heavily, to reduce their own future contingent liabilities. An IFA calculated for me that this bad advice had cost me in excess of £100,000 in lost pension value at retirement and as I have mentioned I have also raised this issue with about **seven regulators, ombudsman or quangos, or**

government helplines, which supposedly exist to benefit the consumer, and all of which are indirectly paid for by tax payers.

Obviously none of them have done anything really meaningful, most have been **useless** – in fact I have been backed up against deadlines so have ended up running out of time – in part because the **agents acting on behalf of the pension trustees intentionally took up lots of time** by delaying replying to letters for as long as possible.

But it was the **Trustees' actions themselves that was most revealing** to me. They rejected my initial claims to them and **refused to answer** some questions (or couldn't answer) and then on appeal they can reassess the case internally **themselves** and of course **find in their own favour**!

What a shock that is.

And they also self-regulate by **deciding themselves that there is no subsequent right of appeal, in any circumstances**. Even state Police Forces like the much maligned Met in London have Independent Complaints Committees – but not pension trustees!

So if you think your trustees' mission in life is to protect pensioners or your pension I would urge you to reconsider and check for yourself, if the main thing they want to achieve is probably to protect their own positions?

Chapter 11

What did I decide to do next?

I think it's fair to say I am in the preparation stage for drawdown so need to get my affairs in order rather than make firm decisions regarding what to do with my pensions going forward. So with this in mind a number of opportunities presented themselves:

Firstly, once you get to within around a year of either your notified possible future retirement age or the standard retirement age, your pension firm will start writing with **reminders**.

They will also send literature from **PensionWise** to help ensure you do not get unwittingly side-tracked by a real scamster who is after your pension proceeds and wants to transfer them somewhere new, earning large fees in the process. This then created an opportunity for a free one-to-one meeting with a PensionWise paid independent advisor (but not a full IFA) with limited knowledge about pensions but able to talk knowledgably about the options and tailor advice to my own personal circumstances – but they give **general** advice rather than **firm** advice.

For the latter, you've guessed it, the advice is talk to an IFA, possibly at a cost of £600 or so unless you buy something in which case it's hidden in the product costs!

So I would conclude that Pension Wise is a bit like talking to the Citizens Advice Bureau, in fact that's where we had our meeting, but overall this was a very good service, and it's free.

So I consider this is a **MUST DO** for anyone's pension planning peace of mind.

Secondly, one thing I noticed was that increasingly the pension funds have **outsourced** their management to huge consulting firms such as Willis Towers Watson, Capita, Sedgewick, and Mercer. As a consequence these companies appear to have standardised ways of working (presumably to increase efficiency and reduce cost) which seem to have reduced some aspects of customer service. So as an example, in the good old days I could request a Pension Transfer Valuation estimate as often as I felt the need and at no charge – now they seem to **limit you to one quote per year**, or **charge**. So I would suggest it's a good idea to get a **rough plan** together **before** wading in and contacting all and sundry about your pensions. These firms also seem pretty good at prevaricating if you ask any difficult questions so I wouldn't expect too much from them in the way of help.

I then decided to **park** for now any attempts to free up my Final Salary pension. It will need sorting eventually because as things stand, when I and my wife die, **nothing passes on to our next of kin,** which is something I would like to fix. In addition, they offer no flexi-access drawdown option – so I have to choose between a poor pension or annuity with them or presumably draw everything out in cash and pay tax at my highest marginal tax rate which is probably 40%. So after the tax free amount this will impact 75% of the funds and that's a lot of tax I don't want to be forced to pay.

I then decided to start **consolidating** the smaller pensions into one pot via a **Self-Invested-Personal-Pension**. I had previously set up a **SIPP** years ago with **JS Bell** who trade as **SippDeal** as they offered at the time amongst the lowest annual charges plus low dealing costs for buying and selling stocks and shares. I decided to check out how big and safe this company was (a bit late in the day admittedly) and decided as they were a privately run company, I wasn't willing to take the risk of putting all my eggs in their particular basket alone, irrespective of whether they are regulated and audited or not.

> **Editor's note** - I guess that confirms a lot about your view of regulators!
>
> **Author's note** – It certainly does and the more I read about the global crash of 2008 and watch the Brexit debacle I'm afraid it just adds to my low opinion about so-called experts.

So back to the plot. I decided to open up a new SIPP with **Hargreaves Lansdown**, notwithstanding that their charges were circa 20% higher for the services I planned to use, as they are one of the biggest companies in the market. Not long after I did this, JS Bell floated on the stock market, I had an offer to subscribe for shares and doubled my money overnight. So whilst that took away my concerns re my former supplier's size and stature it kind of re-affirmed my low opinion of the professionals as whilst they were presumably advised by experts about how much their own company was worth, just 3 months later it was valued at circa 200% of the issue price. If the experts can't advise them properly, what hope have we got with them managing money in our pensions?

Anyway, I've started migrating the smaller pensions to Hargreaves Lansdown with a view to taking 25% out as tax free lump sum and day trading the other 75% in higher dividend paying quality company shares globally....or as I mentioned earlier, my own version of trading which I'm going to christen StayTrading©. So I plan to buy and sell shares in companies like BP, Glaxo, and EasyJet.

The next part of my plan is to transfer my former Final Salary Pension/Mis-sold Money Purchase Plan into another kind of SIPP, but this time after taking out 25% tax free, I plan for it to be invested into a **REIT**, which is a tax free property investment shelter administered through the excellent Bricklane. I like this as whilst it represents further diversification of assets we probably don't need to be wedded to the property as much as we would be if we took the cash out, paid tax, and invested directly in bricks and mortar ourselves.

Workplace Pensions. Whilst the jury is still out as to whether these are really performing as badly as I believe (and they seem destined to mirror the underwhelming performance of Stakeholder pensions whereby 90% didn't even do as well as the FTSE generally) I am evaluating opportunities to keep our scheme open with token payments each month into the old scheme (so it still looks like we have a workplace pension) but instead open up **new SIPPS** for all employees elsewhere with 10% per month contribution (or pay into existing SIPPS) so they can self-manage their funds and hopefully grow at a higher rate.

> **Editor's note** – this seems a lot of hassle? Why not simply close the existing schemes and transfer them to the SIPPs?
>
> **Author's note** – It is, but you can't do that otherwise every 3 years they chase employers, and threaten fines. You then need to set up a new scheme, enrol everyone and they can chose to opt out! It's more jobs for the boys IMHO.
>
> **NB**. I have since discovered that **Nutmeg.com** may provide a route for us to provide an alternative to

a workplace pension with hopefully a greater degree of self-management for staff and better performance prospects than the government run workplace schemes. And it's allowed.

So that's the current plan in progress – at the end of it we should end up with one frozen Final Salary scheme which we will either eventually cash in or drawdown via an annuity, a variety of SIPPS (one for shares the other property), and a yet undecided home for modest workplace pensions.

I will of course in due course take further professional advice from both PensionWise (if they will allow a second meeting) and an IFA, as that may be the route to take out a new pension and at the same time sort out the frozen Final Salary Scheme and decide if an annuity makes sense.

But before I get to that stage I decided I needed to understand more about the various annuity options.

Chapter 12

What are annuities?

I tend to think of Life **Insurance** as a product that typically pays out on a **possible** event, such as death, usually within a pre-agreed **fixed** or limited number of years, so payment out **may** happen, it may not.

In contrast, but similar, there are Assured products such as Life **Assurance**. This has the option to run **forever** and pays out when the event **assured** is to happen, so that could be at the end of a mortgage term or something less positive like death. Payment out then is **guaranteed** hence these kind of products are more expensive.

I think an **Annuity** sits somewhere in the middle but almost in **reverse**. They generally run **forever** (but can be limited) and payments are **guaranteed** for the agreed period or until the known event, death. But unlike Insurance/Assurance where you contribute small sums in each month to get a big pay-out, with an Annuity you **put in the large sum** (from say a maturing pension) and **get small payments back out each month**. These payments out are used as income in retirement and are **generally fixed each month** either **forever** or for a **fixed** period but can also be increased in line with increases in the claimed cost of living.

> **Editor's note** – Why do you say *claimed* cost of living?
>
> **Author's note** – Because Governments are notorious for massaging the figures to make them look good. I suspect the alleged cost of living

increase they announce each year as either RPI or LPI and bears little relation to the real figure out on the streets and even 1% error will hurt when you are on lower incomes like pensions.

I believe I am correct in saying you can buy an annuity with your own spare cash too, called an **Immediate Life Annuity**.

You can also opt to carry across benefits for your **spouse** and other **dependents** after your death but of course each enhancement you make costs the provider (an investment company) more, so they give you **less each month** as your starting pension.

When I started writing this book I had believed that upon death all of the surplus proceeds invested initially into the annuity provider (from your pension) plus any subsequent investment growth they managed to achieve for themselves was always **lost on death** and would not pass to next of kin. This is indeed the case with some Final Salary schemes hence my urgency to move my Bank pension to somewhere I can bequeath or use it. Here in fact is a wording from that pension scheme administrators:

> *Please note that all death benefits are subject to approval from the trustees in the event of your death*

However during the research for the book I came across the **hugely important concept called Capital Protected Annuity** and this is an add-on which can sometimes be purchased when taking out your annuity – basically it guarantees that **whatever is left in the pot** after every beneficiary has died, **gets passed on** to remaining family members. Obviously if the drawings of the beneficiaries of the annuity outlive the pot it's tough luck for the investors providing the annuity (they backed a wrong-un) but there will then be further funds to pass on, even with Capital Protection as all the Capital was used up.

If you don't believe me about how important this aspect of annuities is, here is a **direct quote from LV**, one of the UK's leading Financial Services Companies in March 2019.

If you die, normally your annuity payments will stop and the pension fund used to buy your annuity will be lost.

However there are a number of options you can take to ensure a beneficiary can still benefit from your pension savings or annuity income.

Value protection

Value protection allows you to protect all or part of the fund used to buy your annuity, paying a lump sum outside of your estate.

Guarantee periods

Taking the option of a guaranteed period means you can protect your annuity for a specific number of years and your income will still be paid even if you die before the specified period is up. Selecting a guarantee period will provide a slightly lower level of income, but it guarantees that your estate continues to receive the income.

Joint life annuities

A Joint Life annuity will pay you an income for the rest of your life. It will then go on to pay an income to your spouse, civil partner, or chosen beneficiary for the rest of their life after you die. A beneficiary is someone who is either married to you (including civil partners), your chosen beneficiary or someone who is financially dependent, or dependent due to disability, on you at the date of your death.

It's not easy to get reliable prices on these kind of options and I suspect that's all part of the Pension Pantomime, that is the investors behind annuities **must like it if we fail** to take out any kind of payback option as that's pure profit for them, but more on that in a minute.

> **NB.** I haven't been able to find any data on how many annuities end up running out of beneficiaries before they run out of money (and hence benefit the provider) but I suspect with low awareness it's a very **high proportion of hard-earned money going to waste**.

My researches suggest if I opt for a spouse's pension after I die (at two thirds the level I receive whilst alive) it will drop my own starting pension by about **7% per annum**. So if I was going to get £12,000 annuity pension per year (I wish!), say £1,000 per month, it would drop to £11,160/£930.

If I then want to put a **guarantee** in place, say for 30 years (which should take me past death), it will **cost a further 6%** (or 9% if I omitted the spouse's pension) taking future income down to £874 per month/£10,490 per annum. Conversely a 20 year guarantee would be half this extra cost and a 10 year guarantee seems to be only around **0.25%** cost, a bargain not to be missed!

In summary, it looks to me to be a good deal to Capital Protect your investment fund so your beneficiaries benefit, not the annuity investors or whoever keeps unspent pension money. This is a **relatively new phenomenon only being available for a little over a decade but it's certainly one not to miss, or we're inadvertently being scammed.**

Sadly research from Legal & General suggests that only around a **quarter** of pensioners or those near to pension age are **aware of being able to protect their fund value**. **T**his then seems to be the scam I was worried about when starting to write The Great Pension Pantomime.

In my own case the advisors sub-contracted by my pension funds to advise about annuity options do indeed **mention protection in passing** but they lead with the low cost/statistically-more-likely-to-be-irrelevant short periods such as 10 year guarantees. Any option to ask for much longer or total guarantees is completely **glossed over** and hence almost impossible to take up.

What a poor showing and I can only assume this is intended to boost company profits at the expense of pensioners' families?

Chapter 13

Enhanced Annuities

Another apparent scam is the fact that post people seem to think of pensions in the same way they think of insurance so for example, they **won't be wanting to admit to ill health or a bad lifestyle** in the mistaken belief that this could either get them refused cover (that's the right word if it is insurance) or will reduce the amounts that they can receive in retirement. In actual fact the **reverse is true** as if you have factors that could impact your life (and cut it short) then potentially the pension or annuity provider will have to pay out for a shorter period, and hence they will profit more, particularly if you have failed to take out a capital protection guarantee.

So bad health or a dangerous lifestyle will actually increase the amount your annuity provider will pay out and it's really good to own up to this kind of thing.

As part of my research I decided to put this to the test and as I wanted the largest pay-out possible (only for research purposes, obviously!) I decided to **over-egg** my answers, so as an example I used to smoke as a teenager but probably in reality quit aged around twenty, but as I wasn't precisely sure of the age, I put age 25 years on the enhanced pension quote form….why not!?

And whilst I have various aches and pains and medications that trouble me, these are mostly on an intermittent basis. But I listed everything out on the Enhanced Questionnaire as if it was ongoing so on my enhanced annuity request I suffer from regular migraines, pain in my ankle, undiagnosed kidney problems, fatty liver, you name it. I'm also overweight (and used my weight from a few months back prior to commencing a diet). So I eagerly awaited my enhanced annuity quotation, which was sure to pay me £zillions as I was so poorly?

Guess what, it **increased my pay-out** if I started to collect my pension now aged 60 **by just 1%, that's a grand £55 per annum extra**. What a palaver for nothing. However it has enabled two further interesting bits of research for the book.

Obviously every case is different and I may be far from a typical case but somehow I did my maths magic and was able to work out that this meant the insurers **seemed** to be anticipating I would die roughly aged 82, so the same age as my father.

Secondly, based on the promised annuity for me plus an assumed date of death for my slightly younger wife (who would get a spouse's reduced pension) it looks as if **they would expect to be paying out until 2044**.

And here is the shocker. Even if they stuck our money in a drawer **doing nothing** but gather dust (rather than continued to invest it, which they would) then **our own existing pension pot of money would last until 2042**, just two years short. So in effect the annuity provider would **only need to earn 4.5% on our money in total over 25 years**, to break even, plus costs of course. But this is less than **one twentieth of what inflation might achieve on its own** so hardly speaks volumes for the annuity providers' investment teams.

This is of course unless it's all a scam – if said money **were** invested for this period (as once it's handed over it **becomes their money not our money**, unless I guarantee it with protection of some kind) and just achieved growth equivalent to Base Rate it would increase in value by an estimated **73%**. If as investors we assume they could do better, say 3% **over** Base Rate, they could **grow the money in our pot by a potentially staggering 463%.** I think you will agree that's quite a margin over the less than 5% we need to meet our estimated annuity drawings.

So **maybe that's the Great Pension Pantomime** – most people end up unwittingly leaving money with their pension provider, it goes to waste, and the **pension industry benefits by over 400% of the money entrusted to it?** No wonder some of the key players in the Annuity markets are UK subsidiaries of offshore businesses like Canada Life and ManuLife. I bet they can't get enough of our pensioners' money.

It must seem like Xmas every day of the year to annuity providers?

> **Editor's Note** – It's funny that you should say that – I recall a few years back reading that after a particularly bad stock market slump the spotlight was put onto annuity companies in the context of could they still meet their obligations? The answer from one of them then was that *they were fine; they even had enough spare assets to cope in a once-in-**200-year** disaster scenario*, whatever that means!

So I next decided to run some scenarios that put all this theory to a bit of an unscientific test. I wanted to know what a badly invested annuity might cost me?

Chapter 14

Possible Annuity Scenarios?

I decided to try and estimate forward what would happen if I entered the world of pensions again, so turned the clock back to being 30 in 2018, and armed with the knowledge I now think I've gained, what could happen under certain scenarios?

> **Editor's note** – Why?
>
> **Author's note** - My thinking being that this could make for an interesting read but would also help inform my own decisions about what this would mean for my maturing pension fund projecting forward in time.

I was interested to try and work out:

What would happen if **instead** of a pension I simply **saved up** the money myself to build a pot for retirement versus **how well a pension fund might do** if I invested the recommended amounts and it did as well in the future as my personal pensions (on average) appear to have done for me – so circa 10% per annum growth.

What would that pot look like?

And then when it comes to maturity and retirement, how much might an annuity be and how might that **compare to average wages** in the future?

And **what would I lose if I didn't protect the annuity** somehow? In other words how much **profit might the annuity providers make out of my unintentional misfortune?**

And finally, what if I used a pension as a way of saving (given the generous tax relief at present) **but instead of an annuity, I opted to then self-manage** the resulting fund via something akin to a SIPP today?

To do all these calculations I did of course need to make some important and hard to predict **assumptions** about:

- About both future interest rates and average wages
- Typical wage growth
- Future likely retirement age.

Inflation is of course close to an all time low at present so for that part of the projections I used research from government sources for example for the next few years' predictions and then simply increased the rate each year going forward in linear fashion, so it's clear and simple, albeit it will be inaccurate of course. Interestingly, this still doesn't hit anything like as high a percentage as I encountered when I started work (at around 16%) so my forward prediction suggesting rates might reach the heady levels of **10% or thereabouts by the end of this century** doesn't seem so far fetched as to be implausible?

Average wages are assumed to grow by said **inflation** rate plus I factored in an **assumed promotion every three years** and a resulting extra wage **increase when this happens of 8%** as both these seem to reflect the normal trend, on average.

Retirement age is a tough one to predict – it seems likely the government would keep being forced to push this back as it becomes ever more clear that the country simply can't afford to pay its way and keep rewarding pensioners, but this strategy only works if life expectancy also keeps rising – which it has for the last century. However for the last few years the **average life expectancy** in Europe and particularly in the UK **has been dropping**, presumably due to obesity. This makes the future scenario for pensions even worse so let's look on the bright side.

So I have assumed that **scientific gains** in the health industry will eventually help to redress this balance, people will start living longer again and hence retirement ages can indeed be pushed back. So I don't think it's particularly unrealistic to suggest that somebody aged 31 today will be expected to work until they are **75 years old**, versus 65 today but expected to rise to 67 in the next decade.

> **NB** – I expect this to be pushed back further in this period. This of course is when a State Pension might kick in; a personal pension can be triggered early under current legislation.

And I have stuck with the assumption that somebody starting to save for a pension at age 30 should start with 30 x 0.5 = **15%** of salary, for life.

So who knows if these are a fair assessment or not? What I can say is if I am being overly optimistic here then that's particularly worrying as the numbers don't stack up that well and a pessimistic approach will make everything far worse. So if for example people in future years retire earlier than I have suggested, the pension funds will have an even bigger shortfall, surely?

So has does the data stack up?

	Average Wages Estimate	Inflation Estimate	Salary Increased c3 years @ 8%	Age	Retirement Age Estimate	Contribution %	Contribution Per Year	
2019	£ 28,914	1.0%	£ 28,914	31	65	15%	£ 4,337	Working
2025	£ 31,120	1.6%	£ 36,532	37	68	15%	£ 5,480	Working
2030	£ 34,023	2.1%	£ 46,816	42	69	15%	£ 7,022	Working
2035	£ 38,120	2.6%	£ 61,480	47	71	15%	£ 9,222	Working
2040	£ 43,764	3.1%	£ 76,601	52	72	15%	£ 11,490	Working
2045	£ 51,477	3.6%	£ 105,604	57	73	15%	£ 15,841	Working
2050	£ 62,030	4.1%	£ 149,144	62	74	15%	£ 22,372	Working
2055	£ 76,563	4.6%	£ 199,770	67	75	15%	£ 29,965	Working
2060	£ 96,788	5.1%	£ 295,973	72	75	15%	£ 44,396	Working
2065	£ 125,304	5.6%	£ 449,056	77	75	0%	£ -	Pensioner
2070	£ 166,108	6.1%	£ 645,959	82	75	0%	£ -	Pensioner
2075	£ 225,452	6.6%	£ 1,027,440	87	75	0%	£ -	Pensioner
2080	£ 313,263	7.1%	£ 1,672,979	92	75	0%	£ -	Pensioner
2085	£ 445,599	7.6%	£ 2,581,866	97	75	0%	£ -	Dead / Spouse Pension
2090	£ 648,630	8.1%	£ 4,404,399	102	75	0%	£ -	Dead / Spouse Pension
2095	£ 966,357	8.6%	£ 7,689,156	107	75	0%	£ -	Next of Kin
2100	£ 1,473,263	9.1%	£ 12,718,620	112	75	0%	£ -	Next of Kin

In the table above (which is an extract of every 5 years of data that I have extrapolated to the end of this century) you can see that an average wage today of £28,900 reaches a staggering **£300,000 by the time our imaginary pensioner dies** or a similar amount when they **stop working** (after allowing for inflation and promotions). This will have increased to around £500,000 by the time the spouse dies too at which point somebody still in work could be earning £3m or thereabouts, proving the impact and importance of understanding inflation.

And by the end of the century a typical average wage might be almost 50x higher at £1.5m per annum. Food for thought.

I estimate a projected state retirement at about aged 75, so 2063 by which point they will be saving almost **£45,000 per annum** for retirement and would have put aside around **£150,000**. This will then be used to fund a retirement for pensioner and spouse over the next two decades before hopefully leaving something for next-of-kin.

So with these benchmark numbers as our assumptions let's now look at the various scenarios that could result:

Self-Investing

In the table below I have estimated what would happen if this level of savings were invested/saved yourself rather than handed across to a pension fund. So that could be via investment through say a SIPP (so tax relief is obtained), an ISA or similar, or maybe via a High Interest Savings Account or product like Zopa. Again each row in the chart covers a five year period.

SELF INVESTED @+3% BR	Less Drawings (Optional)	Left Self Invested (For Descendents)	% of Avg Wage	
£ 8,980		£ 8,980		Working
£ 46,365		£ 46,365		Working
£ 95,299		£ 95,299		Working
£ 170,425		£ 170,425		Working
£ 287,747		£ 287,747		Working
£ 475,046		£ 475,046		Working
£ 776,609		£ 776,609		Working
£ 1,269,209		£ 1,269,209		Working
£ 2,089,411		£ 2,089,411		Working
£ 3,265,205	£ 608,008	£ 2,579,016	170%	Pensioner
£ 5,000,899	£ 1,238,418	£ 2,404,610	168%	Pensioner
£ 7,836,694	£ 1,250,000	£ 2,186,257	126%	Pensioner
£ 12,563,758	£ 1,386,337	£ 1,748,240	101%	Pensioner
£ 20,604,550	£ 1,653,862	£ 702,131	87%	Dead / Spouse Pension
£ 34,563,610	£ 663,175	£ 172,386	87%	Dead / Spouse Pension
£ 59,298,444		£ 295,752		Next of Kin
£ 104,038,001		£ 518,891		Next of Kin

Enough left for a deposit on a house?

I estimate the £150,000 invested at just +3% over our estimated Base Rate would **have built up to a fund of £2m** at the point of retirement and circa **£12m on death** (if no drawings were taken) and maybe as much as **£30m by the time a spouse died** (again if no drawings are taken). But taking no money out isn't the purpose of pension savings so let's take out drawings each year, starting at **170% of the average wage** on retirement, dropping to the average wage at death and two thirds for a spouse. So these are quiet generous amounts, that is higher than a Mexican pensioner, but note how they are a lot less than what the wage might really be after allowing for promotions which could be 500% higher.

So in the first 5 years of retirement **£608,000** would be withdrawn to live on (equivalent to circa 1.7X the estimated average wage at the time, and this might be an acceptable income for most people), rising to **£1.3m** over the 5 years when our pensioner probably dies. The balance of the fund of course remains invested throughout.

I estimate that **the money left in the fund** after the pensioner and spouse have died, or at the end of the century, will be roughly enough for our pensioners' next of kin to afford a **deposit on an average priced house.**

> **NB**. Average houses will probably be £14m by then!

In short, it's looking **pretty good for the self-investment** strategy, or is it?!

> **Editor's Note** – I just knew you'd have a sting in the tail somewhere!
>
> **Author's note** – Indeed!

Using a Pension Instead

Obviously I have to assume the investment in a pension will perform close to my average of 10% per annum growth as it's my pretend money I'm interested in working with here!

STD PENSION @10% pa	ANNUITY OPTION (No Capital Protection)	% of Avg Wage	Your Fund Value	Whats Really Left?	
£9,071			£9,071	£9,071	Working
£56,954			£56,954	£56,954	Working
£132,791			£132,791	£132,791	Working
£265,587			£265,587	£265,587	Working
£494,581			£494,581	£494,581	Working
£886,376			£886,376	£886,376	Working
£1,549,288			£1,549,288	£1,549,288	Working
£2,664,340			£2,664,340	£2,664,340	Working
£4,535,394			£4,535,394	£4,535,394	Working
£7,450,327	£562,953	158%		£6,798,146	Pensioner
£11,998,826	£938,254	127%		£9,745,574	Pensioner
£19,324,230	£938,254	95%		£14,492,435	Pensioner
£31,121,865	£938,254	60%		£22,137,303	Pensioner
£50,122,075	£806,899	27%	Nil?	£34,594,259	Dead / Spouse Pension
£80,722,103	£243,946	24%	Nil?	£55,356,426	Dead / Spouse Pension
£130,003,755			Nil?	£89,152,078	Next of Kin
£209,372,347			Nil?	£143,580,913	Next of Kin

Nothing left for family but enough for TEN homes outright for the decendents of the Annuity providers!

As you can see in the table above, the same amount of money invested into my average pensions would have reached **double (at £4.5m)** at the point of retirement and if untouched, **circa £31m (versus just £12m if self-managed)** by estimated time of death.

This is a **very significant improvement on a DIY approach** and calls into question my whole original belief that saving in a pension is a scam.

I have then assumed that an **annuity is taken** on very similar terms to those I am currently being offered so our initial drawings are similar at £560,000 or 1.58X the estimated average wage at retirement. But as the annuity in this case is not index linked, the payments at death are circa 40% lower and at the time of a spouse's death a whole two-thirds worse off and I **can't imagine how a spouse** could hope to manage on just 24% of the estimated average wage then.

> **NB.** I have assumed here that the annuity is unprotected and has no guarantees, so any subsequent upside from ongoing investment will benefit the annuity supplier.

Whereas in a self-managed approach our next of kin might have enough left for at least a deposit on a new home, **if we opt for an unprotected annuity I estimate £22m would be left in the fund on the pensioner's death, growing to circa £50m when the spouse dies and a whopping £143m at the turn of the century.**

So forget leaving behind deposits on your next-of-kins' homes for them, get all this Pension Pantomime wrong and you could just be **leaving enough money on the table to buy the annuity company directors' TEN children each a home, paying for each of them outright** with your hard earned money!

Index Linking

If we used the same approach but linked the future annuity drawings closer to the average wage so our pensioner and spouse can at least have some chance of affording a future lifestyle, what does that look like?

In the table that follows the investment performance is the same, that is within the pension, but the drawings at pension age are index linked to remain at say 1.7X the estimated average wage at the time, so much more liveable albeit not matching pay rising with promotions.

FLEXI PENSION @10% pa	INDEX-LINKED DRAWDOWN	% of Avg Wage	SURPLUS LEFT INVESTED Your Fund Left?	
£ 9,071			£ 9,071	Working
£ 56,954			£ 56,954	Working
£ 132,791			£ 132,791	Working
£ 265,587			£ 265,587	Working
£ 494,581			£ 494,581	Working
£ 886,376			£ 886,376	Working
£ 1,549,288			£ 1,549,288	Working
£ 2,664,340			£ 2,664,340	Working
£ 4,535,394			£ 4,535,394	Working
£ 7,450,327	£ 594,681	167%	£ 6,763,748	Pensioner
£ 11,998,826	£ 1,243,238	168%	£ 9,316,600	Pensioner
£ 19,324,230	£ 1,680,424	168%	£ 12,875,531	Pensioner
£ 31,121,865	£ 2,325,416	169%	£ 17,792,706	Pensioner
£ 50,122,075	£ 3,294,216	170%	£ 24,489,280	ead / Spouse Pension
£ 80,722,103	£ 1,695,191	170%	£ 36,957,107	ead / Spouse Pension
£ 130,003,755			£ 59,519,790	Next of Kin
£ 209,372,347			£ 95,857,217	Next of Kin

Enough to buy SIX houses outright for YOUR decendents?

As you would expect this chops between 25-35% off the fund amounts left invested at various time points but still leaves enough in the pot (if this is an unprotected annuity) to potentially purchase **SIX properties outright for the annuity provider's children**.

Better still, **protect the annuity and those surplus funds could buy a few houses for your own next of kin**. I have already mentioned that costs for this are hard to obtain but if we assume a 30 year period should be enough to take most people up into their 90s (and may cost around 6% of the annuity) then we would still have enough left for **almost six houses for our own next of kin** instead of the annuity providers'!

So **index linking looks attractive provided we also protect the annuity**.

Pension + Self-Management

This then left me with another scenario as with all the new pension freedoms it's possible to use a pension to save up for your retirement but then on reaching the required maturity or State Pension Age you have **freedoms** to chose what to do with your money. One option of course is to cash in the lot and pay a lot of **tax** on most of it, so let's discount that straight away as even invested in property it looks less likely to beat pension returns than I anticipated.

So I thought let's looks at the combined effect of using a **pension to save and self-managing the funds afterwards** when reaching retirement age and taking drawings at a lower level than Index Linked – so the same as the Self Investing scenario at the start.

And this is what it looks like:

PENSION TILL RETIRE THEN SELF MANAGE	Less Drawings (Optional)	% of Avg Wage	SURPLUS LEFT INVESTED Your Fund Left?	LOCATION OF FUNDS	
£ 9,071			£ 9,071	In Pension	Working
£ 56,954			£ 56,954	In Pension	Working
£ 132,791			£ 132,791	In Pension	Working
£ 265,587			£ 265,587	In Pension	Working
£ 494,581			£ 494,581	In Pension	Working
£ 886,376			£ 886,376	In Pension	Working
£ 1,549,288			£ 1,549,288	In Pension	Working
£ 2,664,340			£ 2,664,340	In Pension	Working
£ 4,535,394			£ 4,535,394	In Pension	Working
£ 7,450,327	£ 608,008	170%	£ 5,915,339	In SIPP	Pensioner
£ 11,998,826	£ 1,238,418	168%	£ 6,312,284	In SIPP	Pensioner
£ 19,324,230	£ 1,250,000	126%	£ 6,816,260	In SIPP	Pensioner
£ 31,121,865	£ 1,386,337	101%	£ 7,328,509	In SIPP	Pensioner
£ 50,122,075	£ 1,653,862	87%	£ 7,671,587	In SIPP	Dead / Spouse Pension
£ 80,722,103	£ 663,175	67%	£ 9,205,126	In SIPP	Dead / Spouse Pension
£ 130,003,755			£ 12,030,732	In SIPP	Next of Kin
£ 209,372,347			£ 15,723,685	In SIPP	Next of Kin

Enough to buy ONE average priced house outright for YOUR decendents?

The same £4m fund and drawings at average wage or above and dropping to two thirds for the spouse. The funds then switch to a SIPP which I estimate will grow at roughly half the rate my pension funds achieved. This then leads to a **fund remaining of circa £15m which seems a lot today but in reality is the equivalent of buying just ONE house for your descendants.**

So **not such a good deal after all**, and this was originally my intention before researching to write this book. In fact having now moved a lot of my pensions into a SIPP I think I need to **rethink this strategy seriously and consider re-investing or taking a protected Annuity.**

So what's the conclusion from these scenarios?

Again, please remember this is not advice and I am only projecting forward based on my own experience as if I were starting again for my own family at age 30.

It seems to me though to be a pretty **clear cut case to use pensions to save up** for retirement due in part to all that

tax relief given by the government and this makes it a strong contender versus self-managing your money, as even compared to my own good performance it's harder to beat than you'd think.

My research then seems to point to using a pension to save as a good way forward, then shift to a **flexi-drawdown arrangement** (where you decide how much to take out each year) but **leave the money invested in the pension** and ensure it can pass to your next of kin.

In the table that follows I have summarised what I think might happen plus shown how much could be left on the table due to bad decisions plus how much can be taken off of it each month to live on in retirement.

Confusing or what!

AGE	SELF INVESTED @+5% BR	INTO A PENSION	DRAWINGS AS % AVG WAGE PLUS ANY CASH LEFT?				
			SELF INVESTED	PENSION + ANNUITY	PENSION + FLEXI	PENSION + SIPP	
31	£ 8,980	£ 9,071					Working
37	£ 46,365	£ 56,954					Working
42	£ 95,299	£ 132,791					Working
47	£ 170,425	£ 265,587					Working
52	£ 287,747	£ 494,581					Working
57	£ 475,046	£ 886,376					Working
62	£ 776,609	£ 1,549,288					Working
67	£ 1,269,209	£ 2,654,340					Working
72	£ 2,089,411	£ 4,535,394					Working
77	£ 3,265,205	£ 7,450,327	170%	158%	167%	170%	Pensioner
82	£ 5,000,899	£ 11,998,826	168%	127%	168%	168%	Pensioner
87	£ 7,836,694	£ 19,324,230	126%	95%	168%	126%	Pensioner
92	£ 12,563,758	£ 31,121,865	101%	60%	169%	101%	Pensioner
97	£ 20,604,550	£ 50,122,075	87%	27%	170%	87%	Dead / Spouse Pension
102	£ 34,563,610	£ 80,722,103	67%	24%	170%	67%	Dead / Spouse Pension
107	£ 59,298,444	£ 130,003,755					Next of Kin
112	£ 104,038,001	£ 209,372,347					Next of Kin
		Whats Left?	£ 518,891	Nil?	£ 95,857,217	£ 15,723,685	
			+Deposit	Bad if not Protected	Six Houses?	+House	

The alternative strategy is presumably taking an index linked annuity but again ensuring the surplus can pass onto your kids – but this assumes that the unused annuity remains invested and I won't know the answer to this conundrum probably until I start cashing in my pensions, so will do an update then.

Chapter 15

Other Lessons Learned

The following are a list of observations following all my research to understand my own family pension situation plus research this book:

The **companies keep changing** – as companies shift assets, change names and acquire each other. It's really hard to work out who is really managing your pension and it may no longer be who you think it is. And let's face it, how many of us read every circular they send out, particularly if it's electronic and gets caught by a spam filter.

Time your Transfer Values – I thought it made little difference when I sent in the paperwork to transfer out money. But it does. I inadvertently sent in papers for one of mine without checking in advance the transfer value, so I assumed its value based on where it had historically been, and it **lost circa 5% value overnight**.

Slow at Admin - Also not all companies process paperwork at the same rate – this particular company closed down my pension within one day, others have taken a month or longer. I think that's slightly suspicious but how do I prove it?

Beware Government Schemes – Despite having good intentions in the majority of cases these schemes don't seem to achieve the market average, but it's hard to tell for sure when in the early years a large proportion of assets goes into paying management fees.

Watch out for Fees, both upfront and ongoing. Good advice costs so having fees is no bad thing provided you get the performance and support to compensate. But as fees can impact the outcome (in my case by 10%) it's worth checking you are paying appropriate amounts at all times.

Carefully check Performance – It's easy to make a snap assessment about how an investment such as a pension is performing by either taking too much or not enough notice of one year's figures versus the next. I think it's a great idea to **map the trends** and compare this performance with the broader market's, plus of course check those fees as a proportion too.

Don't get Fined – As an employer you will get fined if you don't take your workers' pension rights seriously so there is no point trying to duck responsibility for them and yourself. And if you don't, the government are quick to send out fine notices – we had one even though we were one of the first companies in the UK to set up a workplace pension voluntarily.

Mixed Blessings of Final Salary Schemes – These are generally great if you have one and a lot of years under your belt but they are almost impossible to get out of (into something more flexible) due to all the fear of being sued.

It's all a Pantomime – picking a good pension provider seems to me to be a complete pantomime, maybe even a **lottery**, as how can you sort the good from the bad when they all have to quote **standardised performance** figures for future growth using fixed percentages? And as an industry there is so much smoke and mirrors with information overload (even from non IFAs who can't advise so just provide all the data so you can make an informed choice) that it's almost impossible to see the wood for the trees, even if you have half an idea what you are looking for. To me this suggests the best plan is to **pick several**

horses in the race and then benchmark them at regular intervals, killing off the poor performers.

Fix your mistakes, quickly – I have unwittingly:

- Paid too much in fees for mediocre levels of advice (discovered after the event)
- I have switched funds (without checking the balance that day)
- I have been miss-sold too and then let trustees back me up against the wall (running out of time)
- I have tracked performance but failed to map it out properly to compare with others.

In combination these errors have cost me maybe **30% of my pension** pot and could all have been remedied by greater attention to detail and faster action. It's too late after the event – I'm fortunate that overall these mistakes have only added up to about 5% of my total retirement income, it could have been so much worse if I hadn't spent that time wisely elsewhere.

Chapter 16

The Future?

Quite where all this research leaves our family personally is hard to say exactly. We are midway through successfully merging all our smaller pensions into a much smaller array of pots to keep an eye on, and if I get the chance I may also try and bring my small workplace pension into one of these so we have less hassle.

At the present time that leaves me with an **orphaned** Final Salary Scheme to still resolve, I am not willing to waste 1% of that scheme's value on advice I don't need, but equally I don't see why I should be forced to take cash (and pay a high rate of tax on the proceeds) to get the freedom I desire so we can leave money for our next of kin after we die.

This probably will push us into a chat with a friendly and helpful IFA?

That then leaves the largest pension pot in a SIPP which in turn is invested in **property**, and I've chosen this intentionally as the property markets are down (and I fear the stock market is long overdue another big crash) so I suspect as the bulk of the REIT income derives from property rentals (which never seem to go down, even in a recession) this might be a good **hedge against the markets**, notwithstanding a general over exposure to property in our portfolio generally. So it will be hugely interesting to see how this performs and no doubt I can opt back out of property at a later date if needed or after substantive returns are made by simply switching say to another SIPP, but not a property one.

Then we have another substantial SIPP (the accumulation of most of the smaller pensions) that is currently being invested in **stocks and shares**, mostly in the UK (whilst that market is deflated due to Brexit) plus around 20% overseas in blue-stock shares. A difficulty in trading these is a 2% extra charge to cover currency conversion. I had planned to make **DIY investing of said shares a firm part of my ongoing pension plan** (after taking out 25% tax free) but now that I have written this Bite-Sized book I have to seriously question and **challenge the wisdom** of this – **would it not be better to try and reinvest the money into a new pension** to take advantage of a hoped for 10% per annum growth?

I had previously thought the answer to this would be a clear **No**, as my own share trading seems to yield over 12% generally (albeit the current run rate over the last 18 months' trading is nearer **21% per annum from share trading**) and is hence even better than my general pension experience, so why not simply keep doing that as it takes a few minutes each day?

But there is a proviso to be added to this, and an important one. At the time of writing the total value of my SIPP portfolio is **down circa 3%** versus the input cash 3 months ago and yet on paper my profits should make it **3% up**. Until I can resolve this possibly theoretical but potentially vitally important paper or mathematical anomaly I **can't say for sure that my trading beats pensions**. When I know I can move forward with meetings with an IFA or more share trading.

      Editor's note – That is odd isn't it.

Author's note – It is. I think the explanation is that in the past I've day traded equities (or as I call it, StayTraded©) with a fund of about £30,000 but now that I am expanding this activity to take account of all my pension assets, it involves owning a much bigger portfolio of shares, so say, shares in 50 companies instead of just 10. Whilst this should be a good thing as it **spreads risk** and increases the opportunity to take profits every day (hence why I think I've made 3%), to end up 3% down, maybe the **rest of the portfolio is down 6% in the same period?** If these losing stocks eventually come good and eventually make money, it could indeed be a winning strategy and worthy of a book, but if they don't come good and I'm **stuck with lots of underperforming shares in loss** I will have to rethink my DIY investing pension plan.

Hopefully though the test won't have lost all my money in the same way that gambling on horses might!

Chapter 17

Summary

Let's wrap up this Bite Sized Book on pensions then with my summary.

I started out in the very clear **initial** belief that the whole pension scene is little more than a **scam**, a pantomime if you will juggling advisors, bad performance, high fees and ultimately inflexible annuities that see money wasted when you die. It seemed likely to be a scam everyone should **avoid** and I was disheartened that I was at the heart of it trying to plan a retirement, by which point of course it's mostly too late.

But **what I discovered is mostly the opposite of this.**

Yes it's true that high fees can be paid and some companies appear to overcharge over others, but **performance generally turned out to be good** – provided you look over the **long-term**, which is important.

Schemes encouraged by **government** seem likely to be poor value, but again with a caveat, have we really been **investing for long enough** to make that prediction? Possibly not.

So **pension saving with hindsight does seem to be a good thing** (assuming our family experiences are broadly typical) and would seem to make more sense than saving under the mattress or even trying to manage your own funds via high interest earning savings accounts or a DIY investment approach. And of course a big part of this success must be down to the **generous tax relief**/free contribution made by the government by adding £1 for free to every £4 you invest yourself.

Annuities have of course fared less well in the analysis.

Given the discovery that over the last decade or so pension freedoms have not only increased the choices regarding what you must **do** with a maturing pension fund but have also enabled protection or guarantees re **where** the money ends up - so after your death any unused portion **no longer needs to go to waste**. Sadly this seems to be little publicised and this then seems to be **where the Great Pension Pantomime may be hiding the real scam?** – People that don't read and understand the fine print may **miss this opportunity to protect their money**, leaving huge fortunes and profits on the table for annuity providers instead of their own next of kin.

And who wants to die knowing they've enabled already rich shareholders' families somewhere to buy another ten houses outright when probably their own grandchildren won't even have the deposit for a home of their own? I know we didn't expect that outcome and **we weren't even aware the choice existed.**

I have no way of knowing for sure how accurate this scenario is but for me it's certainly **food for thought** and has made us rethink how we exit our pensions or indeed if we do so at all. One important aspect of this of course is that money in a pension is currently treated differently when you die to money taken out and left in your estate generally, so it's important to make the right choice informed with the best knowledge available, including **inheritance tax** issues, of which I currently know almost less than nothing. But hopefully our experiences with at least the Pension part of the Pantomime helps point readers in the right direction or frame of mind to ask more questions.

We've learnt the hard way that the regulators and trustees are probably not on your side as much as you'd like to think but then due to various regulatory rules and commission arrangements, it's probable that neither are the Independent Financial Advisors we think we can trust. So this makes people like **PensionWise more important than ever** and everyone should ensure they have a chat with these folks, for free.

We've also learnt not just the importance of checking small-print and notices from the financial providers regularly, but it also seems a great idea to **record and plot out** in a graph or simple table how well investments are doing so you can compare them with each other and **benchmark** against other performance measures such as the global stock markets, funds in general or any specialist area if that's what you've chosen to focus your investment strategy on, for example China, Emerging Nations, Technology, Bio-Sciences.

That then leads to the final conclusion – not only are pensions (and what you do with the money saved up) the Great Pension Pantomime as predicted, it also seems very much a **lottery**. I can't think of any really reliable way to predict which is a good or bad company and hence the best advice seems to me to be to **spread the risk** and save in multiple different pension pots – maybe switching funds when one is plainly consistently underperforming over a few years or seems to be overcharging. This then makes it important to **understand any barriers** or charges to exit and move money around.

So that's it – it does seem as if **Pensions are indeed a Pantomime** and just like working out how a stage magician does his or her tricks, it's not easy to fathom the world of pensions which gets ever more complex year after year. I do hope though that our experiences help you with your own journey into this part of the weird world of money.

Happy Pension Planning.

Stuart Haining, Northampton. April 2019

Footnote

I will revisit this section if we ever get to the bottom of what to do with that stuck Final Salary Scheme or understand whether a new pension is better (with a flexi drawdown arrangement) than taking an annuity with a guarantee.

One extra thing I have learnt is it seems to be a good idea to suddenly **ramp up our pension contributions before we start undertaking any drawdown**, this way we have the option of re-investing a greater proportion of our tax free cash than if we kept our contributions low or nil, as might be typical. This is because you can't put more into a pension at drawdown than you did when you were working – or something like that!

The next bit of extra news to add post completion of this Bite-Sized Book then is that I have subsequently contacted Pension Wise to see if it is indeed acceptable to have a **second face to face consultation** with them Free of charge. I'm pleased to report they are very on-the-ball answering queries and I had a positive response to my email within a day. The less good news is that the service is **very popular** – so the first available appointment is **FIVE weeks away**, in this area anyway, so the moral of this particular story is don't leave arranging your Pension Wise meeting until the last minute, such as before a deadline. And as before my meeting will be at the local Citizens Advice offices.

It's prudent I think to take an updated list of all your pensions (transfer amounts and maturity dates) plus balances for any other assets held, loans, regular income and of course outgoings so as to be prepared for most questions they may ask.

I will provide a further update in due course hopefully after the next review meeting with them and possibly an IFA.

The second meeting with Pension Wise proved to be just as useful as the first so **using this FREE service is a strong recommendation for everyone**, whatever the state of your pension arrangements. So what have I learnt:

- If I inadvertently selected a bad annuity option there is a 30 day **cooling off** period, not long of course but better than nothing!
- Taking the **25% tax-free is not counted as a trigger event**, so you are not in drawdown. Take 25.1% and you would be, this then has an impact on all manner of things, such as determining how much you can keep adding to your pension each year and still get tax relief. (A **£4,000 limit** usually kicks in).
- Pension **contributions can be 100% of your total income**, so that's not just your income from work, or up to £40,000 per annum, whichever is **lowest**. I didn't realise **secondary income could be taken into account** so this lifts our possible pension contributions by about 40%.
- I've re-affirmed that if you plan to keep paying into a pension it's important to increase your contributions well in advance of drawdown or taking 25% tax free otherwise the tax man may decide you are illegally **recycling** money and will charge **55% tax as a penalty**. I think we will simply stop contributing and buy a new car.

- There are three ways of getting some kind of protection with an annuity, firstly having a **Joint Life** so it pays for longer, secondly a **Guarantee** for a specific number of years that payments will be made for, and thirdly ensuring you ask for **Value Protection to be added in**. This seems to me to be the best option but may be the most expensive as it's robbing them of ten free houses! (as outlined in the book).
- It is vital to complete a **Nomination of Benefits Form** regarding where you **wish** your pension to go after your death, and for this to be at the **discretion** of the pension trustees (who shouldn't ignore a reasonable bequest). This discretion makes it sit **outside your estate** when you die (so under current regulations **saves inheritance tax**) whereas if you make it a straight demand regarding where the funds go, they will go there, but it **will be taxed** as part of the estate. So discretionary seems important.
- Finally, not really relevant to me but a **Final Salary** scheme will be valued for purposes of deciding whether you have exceeded the maximum you can have in a pension pot (£1m+) by **multiplying the annual pension payments by 20**, so they assume you will live 20 years. This values mine at about £60,000 so that's similar to the cash transfer value and nowhere near enough to pose a problem, sadly!

Latest update (May 2019) is that despite the provider of the Final Salary Scheme saying it is unimportant if the advice to swap is negative, that is, the advisor doesn't agree, that doesn't matter – it's taking advice that counts and at the end of the day it is your own money to do with as you wish. That seems fair but surprising. However, getting a scheme to accept a transfer in seems impossible as they will only do so if the IFA advice is in favour, even if you offer them a letter indemnifying them against any future compensation claims. And of course the Pension Regulator will do nothing to help in terms of an adjudication or anything else as "it's beyond our remit"

So the words rock and hard place come to mind.

That's it for now but I will update the book if anything spectacular happens in a meeting with an **IFA**, I do need to have one as Pension Wise (other than the above nugget of information) won't or can't discuss FS schemes under their remit from the government, but they are trained to discuss most other things.

Bite-Sized Business Books are designed to provide support and insights for professionals who are tackling an unfamiliar task either for the first time or after a gap, as well as those who want to find new ways of doing what they are familiar with.

They are deliberately short, easy to read, step-by-step manuals and books guiding the reader through the various stages behind each business process or activity, with a clear focus on outcomes. They are firmly based on personal experience and success.

The most successful people all share an ability to focus on what really matters, keeping things simple and understandable. MBAs, metrics and methodologies have their place, but when we are faced with a new challenge most of us need quick guidance on what matters most, from people who have been there before and who can show us where to start. As Stephen Covey famously said, "The main thing is to keep the main thing, the main thing".

But what exactly is the main thing?

Bite-Sized books were conceived to help answer precisely that question crisply and fast and, of course, be engaging to read, written by people who are experienced and successful in their field.

The brief? Distil the "main things" into a book that can be read by an intelligent non-expert comfortably in around 60 minutes. Make sure the book enables the reader with specific tools, ideas and plenty of examples drawn from real life and business. Be a virtual mentor.

Bite-Sized Books don't cover every eventuality, but they are written from the heart by successful people who are happy to share their experience with you and give you the benefit of their success.

We have avoided jargon – or explained it where we have used it as a shorthand – and made few assumptions about the reader, except that they are in business, are literate and numerate, and that they can adapt and use what we suggest to suit their own, individual purposes. Whether you are working for a multi-national corporation or a start-up or something in between, the principles we introduce will hold good.

They can be read straight through at one easy sitting and then used as a support while you are working on what you need to do.

Bite-Sized Books Catalogue

Business Books

Ian Benn
- Write to Win
  - How to Produce Winning Proposals and RFP Responses

Matthew T Brown
- Understand Your Organisation
  - An Introduction to Enterprise Architecture Modelling

David Cotton
- Rethinking Leadership
  - Collaborative Leadership for Millennials and Beyond

Richard Cribb
- IT Outsourcing: 11 Short Steps to Success
  - An Insider's View

Phil Davies
- How to Survive and Thrive as a Project Manager
  - The Guide for Successful Project Managers

Paul Davies
- Developing a Business Case
  - Making a Persuasive Argument out of Your Numbers

Paul Davies
> Developing a Business Plan
>> Making a Persuasive Plan for Your Business

Paul Davies
> Contract Management for Non-Specialists

Paul Davies
> Developing Personal Effectiveness in Business

Paul Davies
> A More Effective Sales Team
>> Sales Management Focused on Sales People

Paul Davies
> The Naked Human in Business
>> Accelerate Your Personal Effectiveness by Understanding Humans – The Practical One Two Three of Business Development

Tim Emmett
> Bid for Success
>> Building the Right Strategy and Team

Nigel Greenwood
> Why You Should Welcome Customer Complaints And What to Do About Them

Nigel Greenwood
> Six Things that All Customer Want
>> A Practical Guide to Delivering Simply Brilliant Customer Service

Stuart Haining
> The Practical Digital Marketeer – Volume 1
>> Digital Marketing – Is It Worth It and Your First Steps

Stuart Haining
> The Practical Digital Marketeer – Volume 2
>> Planning for Success

Stuart Haining
> The Practical Digital Marketeer – Volume 3
>> Your Website

Stuart Haining
> The Practical Digital Marketeer – Volume 4
>> Be Sociable – Even If You Hate It

Stuart Haining
> The Practical Digital Marketeer – Volume 5
>> Your On-going Digital Marketing

Stuart Haining
> Profitable Partnerships
>> Practical Solutions to Help Pick the Right Business Partner

Stuart Haining
> MLM 101
>> The Difficult Questions and Answers Most Networkers Daren't Reveal

Stuart Haining
> The Great Pension Pantomime
>> It's All a Scam – Oh Yes It Is – Oh No It Isn't

Christopher Hosford
> Great Business Meetings! Greater Business Results
>> Transforming Boring Time-Wasters into Dynamic Productivity Engines

Ian Hucker
> Risk Management in IT Outsourcing
>> 9 Short Steps to Success

Alan Lakey
    Idiocy in Commercial Life
        Practical Ways to Navigate through Nonsense
Marcus Lopes and Carlos Ponce
    Retail Wars
        May the Mobile be with You
Maiqi Ma
    Win with China
        Acclimatisation for Mutual Success Doing Business with China
Elena Mihajloska
    Bridging the Virtual Gap
        Building Unity and Trust in Remote Teams
Rob Morley
    Agile in Business
        A Guide for Company Leadership
Gillian Perry
    Managing the People Side of Change
        Ten Short Steps to Success in IT Outsourcing
Art Rain
    The Average Wage Millionaire
        Can Anyone Really Get Rich?
Saibal Sen
    Next Generation Service Management
        An Analytics Driven Approach
Don Sharp
    Nothing Happens Until You Sell Something
        A Personal View of Selling Techniques

Lifestyle Books

Anna Corthout
    Alive Again
        My Journey to Recovery

Anna Corthout
    Mijn Tweede Leven
        Kruistocht naar herstel

Phil Davies
    Don't Worry Be Happy
        A Personal Journey

Phil Davies
    Feel the Fear and Pack Anyway
        Around the World in 284 Days

Stuart Haining
    My Other Car is an Aston
        A Practical Guide to Ownership and Other Excuses to Quit Work and Start a Business

Stuart Haining
    After the Supercar
        You've Got the Dream Car – But Is It Easy to Part With?

Bill Heine
    Cancer
        Living Behind Enemy Lines Without a Map

Regina Kerschbaumer
    Yoga Coffee and a Glass of Wine
        A Yoga Journey

Gillian Perry
    Capturing the Celestial Lights
        A Practical Guide to Imagining the Northern Lights

Arthur Worrell
    A Grandfather's Story
        Arthur Worrell's War

Public Affairs Books

David Bailey, John Mair and Neil Fowler (Editors)
> Keeping the Wheels on the Road – Brexit Book 3
> UK Auto Post Brexit

Eben Black
> Lies Lobbying and Lunch
>> PR, Public Affairs and Political Engagement – A Guide

Paul Davies, John Mair and Neil Fowler
> Will the Tory Party Ever Be the Same? – Brexit Book 4
>> The Effect of Brexit

John Mair and Neil Fowler (Editors)
> Oil Dorado
>> Guyana's Black Gold

John Mair and Richard Keeble (Editors)
> Investigative Journalism Today:
>> Speaking Truth to Power

John Mair and Neil Fowler (Editors)
> Do They Mean Us – Brexit Book 1
>> The Foreign Correspondents' View of the British Brexit

John Mair, Alex De Ruyter and Neil Fowler (Editors)
> The Case for Brexit – Brexit Book 2

John Mair, Richard Keeble and Farrukh Dhondy (Editors)
> V.S Naipaul:
>> The legacy

John Mills
> Economic Growth Post Brexit
>> How the UK Should Take on the World

Christian Wolmar
> Wolmar for London
>> Creating a Grassroots Campaign in a Digital Age

Fiction

Paul Davies
> The Ways We Live Now
>> Civil Service Corruption, Wilful Blindness, Commercial Fraud, and Personal Greed – a Novel of Our Times

Paul Davies
> Coming To
>> A Novel of Self-Realisation

Victor Hill
> Three Short Stories
>> Messages, The Gospel of Vic the Fish, The Theatre of Ghosts

Children's Books

Chris Reeve – illustrations by Mike Tingle
> The Dictionary Boy
>> A Salutary Tale

Fredrik Payedar
> The Spirit of Chaos
>> It Begins

www.ingramcontent.com/pod-product-compliance
Lightning Source LLC
Chambersburg PA
CBHW022110170526
45157CB00004B/1570